Advance Buzz for *Plug Your Book!*

"I don't care if you're writing a computer book, a science fiction novel, or the next great self-help guide, you need to get your hands on a copy of Steve Weber's *Plug Your Book!* I highly recommend this one to every author out there."

— Joe Wikert, executive publisher, John Wiley & Sons Inc., professional/trade division

"An amazingly rich collection of cutting-edge promotional tactics and strategies. Makes most other books about online publicity look sickly."

— Aaron Shepard, author: *Aiming at Amazon*

"In-depth information about using Amazon as a marketing platform."

— Christine McNeil Montano, Amazon Top Reviewer

"...I have launched online campaigns for more than 1,000 books. I've worked with most of America's largest book publishers, helping many of them build online marketing departments. The book you're holding now is the new training manual."

— Steve O'Keefe, author: *Publicity on the Internet*

"Practical, pragmatic, low-cost ideas for promoting the heck out of your own book, whether it's fiction, nonfiction, technical, business or anything else."

— Dave Taylor, author: *The Complete Idiot's Guide to Growing Your Business with Google*

"The first comprehensive guide to Internet book publicity."

— Morris Rosenthal, publisher, Foner Books

"A wealth of ideas for making your book stand out, including many techniques for Internet buzz you won't find elsewhere."

— Jane Corn, Amazon Top Reviewer

Plug Your Book!

Online Book Marketing for Authors
2nd Edition

Weber Books

By Steve Weber

With Laurie Jackson

All Rights Reserved © 2007, 2013 by Stephen W. Weber

Published by Stephen W. Weber

Printed in the United States of America

Weber Books   www.WeberBooks.com

Author: Steve Weber

13-digit ISBN: 978-1-936560-15-8

10-digit ISBN: 1-936560-15-1

Authorship—Marketing

Front cover photo: Copyright JupiterImages Corp.

Back cover photo: Sam Holden Photography

Contents

Warning and Disclaimer

About the author

Steve Weber has been writing about Amazon.com for nearly a decade. He is founding publisher of Kindle Buffet, a website and newsletter that showcases great books available free during temporary promotions. For more information, see:

www.KindleBuffet.com

Preface to the Second Edition

When I wrote *Plug Your Book!* in 2007, it was the first comprehensive book about online book marketing. Things have changed, to put it mildly. Back then, eBooks, Amazon's Kindle, and Facebook weren't even a blip on the radar screen. Many of the details from that first edition were obsolete after just a few short months. But the central philosophy behind *Plug Your Book!* is even more valid today than ever: that online communities have empowered authors as never before. Using the grassroots publicity techniques described in this book, authors can connect directly with readers—a revolutionary development.

It was true then, and it's even more true today. You, the author, are the best advocate for your book. You can market it better than anyone because you know it best.

And the biggest caveat from the original *Plug Your Book!* is still true, too: I can't guarantee you a successful book launch, and nobody else can, either. That still depends on how good your book is, and how good a job you do at promoting it.

As one of my cranky old editors used to say, "You can't make a silk purse out of a sow's ear." Likewise, no fancy online marketing program can breathe success into a crummy book. That's the whole point. The Internet makes it harder and harder to sell stuff that stinks.

With Internet communities, word of mouth is amplified and accelerated. Online buzz makes it easier to sell good stuff, but harder to sell mediocre stuff. Word gets around. For the strategies in this book to work, your book needs to be strong, because your best competitors are online, too.

Internet word of mouth depends on an involved, educated consumer. You're asking your readers to help promote your book, and this requires a *very good* book, according to your audience. *Bad* word of mouth will hurt your sales. Online marketing helps a bad book fail faster.

So it's a double-edged sword. The good news is that, unlike the past, your successful writing career doesn't necessarily depend on having "pull," or special help from publishing bigwigs. It all depends on you—and your readers. And that's just the way it should be.

Foreword

If your book is your business, this is your book.

I have enormous sympathy for authors. Imagine spending months or years putting everything you know into a book, polishing every page to get it *just right,* and just when you thought you were finished—surprise! Now you have to learn everything you never wanted to know about book publishing and marketing.

Today it's not just self-published authors who face this daunting challenge. If you are lucky enough to land a contract with a mainstream book publisher, surprise! The marketing plan is in your mirror—go take a look. That's right, you are responsible for promoting your own book. If you don't, your publisher won't hesitate to replace you on the roster with an author who hustles.

So here you are, book in hand or about to be published, and you're presented with a task that makes writing the book look easy. Your dilemma: How can you connect your book with readers?

Fortunately, the truth is on your side. All marketing boils down to one happy conclusion: in all voluntary transactions, both sides win. I value your book more than my money; you value my money more than the book. We trade. We both walk away richer for the experience.

What that means for marketers is you don't need to con people or hard-sell them. All you have to do is show people the value, and they will gladly trade their dollars for your book.

I've been promoting books online since 1992. In that time, I have launched online campaigns for more than 1,000 books. I've worked with most of America's largest book publishers, helping many of them build online marketing departments. The book you're holding now is the new training manual.

I've worked for dozens of self-published authors, too. Faced with the enormously time-consuming process of online marketing, they usually ask me, "If this were your book, what would you do?" Now here's what I tell them:

First, read Steve Weber's *Plug Your Book!*

Second, make a copy of the table of contents.

Now, cross off each chapter as you complete the task or pass over it.

When you're finished, you've done everything that can reasonably be done to launch a book on the Internet.

If marketing is all about communicating value, what makes Steve Weber's *Plug Your Book!* so valuable? Like publishing gurus Dan Poynter, John Kremer, Judith Appelbaum, Jeff Herman, and John Huenefeld, Steve Weber drills down into the nitty-gritty with the best of them. For example, when he talks about marketing on Facebook, I tingle as he reveals exactly how to process "friend" requests.

That level of detail—such as explaining the difference between Amazon's "Best Value" and "Better Together" programs—is carried through every chapter. Weber has used most of these techniques several times and reports honestly on the results. Yes, marketing your book online is going to take time—you can't phone-in a blog tour—but following Steve Weber's map will save you time. And improve your results. And that adds up to *value* to me.

Steve Weber is hip to what is happening online today—such as social networking, amateur content, and reputation management—and he's got a keen insight into what's coming: swarms of tag clouds devouring video profiles and spitting out serendipitous links. His excitement for sharing these techniques is palpable. His section on Amazon marketing programs is like an M.R.I. exam, poking into every corner of the giant retailer's vast apparatus and finding promotional opportunities at every turn.

Weber's honesty is also commendable, as when he warns marketers against plumping pages with phony reviews and when he exposes the shortcomings of Search Engine Optimization (SEO).

Steve Weber's *Plug Your Book!* won't spare you the plight of all modern authors—having to get out there and push that book. But it will make your time online more productive, more pleasant, and at times, fascinating as all get out!

STEVE O'KEEFE

—NEW ORLEANS

O'Keefe is founder of Patron Saint Productions, a pioneer in providing online video for the book industry. An entrepreneur, writer, and university professor, O'Keefe is the author of five books, is co-founder of the International Association of Online Communicators (IAOC) and teaches Internet Public Relations at Tulane University.

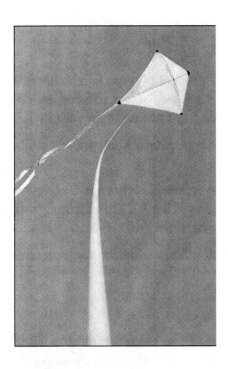

Introduction

No matter what kind of book you have, its success depends on two things: It must tell a good story, and you must find an audience for it. Easier said than done, but you might take a page from master storyteller Hans Christian Andersen.

As legend has it, schoolchildren in Andersen's Danish town played hooky from school just to hear him spin his tales. Each time he felt like telling another one, Andersen signaled his desire by flying his kite. When the kite rose, word spread quickly, and the crowd gathered.

Can it be that simple in today's world? Can the modern author build an audience solely through community word of mouth?

Yes, you can, and you don't even need to leave your backyard. Today's authors can launch their kites to potentially huge audiences by participating in Internet communities. The big difference is, your online community isn't limited to your neighborhood—it can span the globe if you invest in some string.

More than ever, authors and readers are networking, even collaborating on books as peers. With simple Internet tools, determined writers—even beginners working on obscure projects—can find their audience. Using online communities, authors can reach readers directly, bonding intimately, inspiring deep loyalty.

Online social networking has handed authors their most powerful tool since the invention of paper. In the Networked Age, the stock of gatekeepers is going down, and the power of authors and readers is soaring.

Word of mouth is the only thing that can make a book really successful. And this has always been the challenge: How can the author break through? Until recently, it usually required "pull"—connections with powerful allies in the publishing industry. Today, creative writers can connect with readers without special favors from publishing bigwigs. The only requirements are a link to the Internet and the will to plug in.

Taking Control of Your Book Sales

This year, some 200,000 authors will finish their masterpiece, but most of them will be horribly disappointed with the results—only a small percentage of new titles sell more than 100 copies. Yes, most books are unmitigated flops, and the quality of the manuscript often has nothing to do with it.

Most books fail because hardly anyone noticed them. And nowadays, even a high-priced traditional marketing campaign can't prevent a book from flopping.

Old-fashioned marketing and advertising is less effective than ever; people ignore it. But *free* advertising is alive and well, and savvy authors are using it to sell tons of books. The catch is, you can't manufacture free advertising; you must earn it with your own elbow grease.

Now for the first time, authors and readers can ignite word of mouth using online communities to spread the word about good books. It's not rocket science. Anyone with the skills to write an e-mail can publicize their book worldwide, effectively and economically.

How to Use This Book

The beginning sections of this book explain the basics of online book promotion, techniques that provide the most bang for your effort. As we proceed, some of the methods will get more involved, demanding more expertise and time. Perhaps not everything discussed here will be practical for your book.

Your job is to select which promotional techniques might work best with your audience, and then use them aggressively and tirelessly. The more techniques you try, the better your chances of discovering your winning formula. A single idea won't produce a home run, but a combined effort will keep you in the game and the results and effect will be cumulative.

This book is not a quick-fix plan; there is no such thing as overnight success. It might require a year or more of steady work to see appreciable results. If that seems like a gamble and lots of work, it is. But I assure you, it's not nearly as difficult as writing a book.

So, you've finished your book, and that's a tremendous accomplishment. But you're not done yet. You've got more work to do—to ensure your words reach as many people as possible.

I wish you much success in your journey.

—**STEVE WEBER**

Falls Church, Virginia

Electric Word of Mouth

In 1988 a first-time author, British mountaineer Joe Simpson, wrote of his disastrous climbing accident in the Peruvian Andes. His book, *Touching the Void*, got good reviews, but wasn't too popular outside England. It sold modestly and then, like most books, began fading into obscurity.

A decade later, another climbing book was penned by Jon Krakauer, an American journalist who scaled Everest during a harrowing expedition that claimed eight lives. *Into Thin Air*, thanks to a marketing boost from its New York publisher, was an instant No. 1 bestseller and worldwide blockbuster.

And then something really interesting happened. Bookstores started getting requests for the earlier book, *Touching the Void*. Weeks before, booksellers couldn't give the book away, and now it was sold out. Library copies went missing. The original hardback, if you could find one, was selling for $375. Harper Paperbacks quickly printed a new edition, and *Touching the Void* started outselling the new "blockbuster" by two to one.

What happened? Who was the marketing whiz behind this literary resurgence? Actually, it wasn't an organized effort at all. It was a result of the automated book recommendations at Amazon.com. The online store began recommending the older book to millions of people whom it knew liked climbing books, based on their recent purchases. If you've shopped on Amazon, you've seen these recommendations yourself: "People who bought *this book* also bought…"

Many of the new readers liked *Touching the Void* so much, they wrote rave reviews on Amazon's site. These "amateur" book reviews, written by real climbers and armchair explorers, struck a chord with the next wave of shoppers. The result: more sales, more good reviews.

Ten years after the book's launch, Internet-powered word of mouth did something that its publisher could never do—it landed *Touching the Void* on the bestseller lists. The story was adapted for an acclaimed docudrama. Simpson, his writing career energized, followed up with four successful adventure books, a novel and lecture tours.

Today, readers are finally able to find exactly the books they want without consulting a librarian or bookstore clerk. Readers are flocking to Amazon and online reading communities to discover what's worth reading. All this is a godsend for authors, who finally have a way to build their audience effectively and without traditional marketing expenses. Never has it been so practical, so straightforward, so cheap for writers to earn a living at their craft and build a following.

Today, book *readers* are helping decide which books sink or swim. As an author, you can take advantage of this new environment using the techniques described in this book.

Riding the Big River

In its relatively brief lifetime, Amazon.com has helped demolish the walls separating writers and readers. No longer are new authors summarily locked out of the bookstore. Whether your book was trade-published or self-published, whether it's available in hardcover, softcover, eBook or audio—or any combination of the above—Amazon will not only stock it, but *rearrange the whole store* when a likely reader arrives. And if your book sells modestly well, Amazon will do lots more—like displaying your book right inside the door, at the end of each virtual aisle, on eight different category shelves, and smack-dab in front of the cash register. Think your local bookstore might do this? Maybe if you're William Shakespeare, but the rest of us are out of luck.

Book sales over the Internet now account for more than half the receipts of traditional publishers. The share claimed by eBooks is rising fast, now accounting for about 20 percent of overall sales, compared to virtually nothing just a few years ago, according to the Book Industry Study Group. Amazon, with its Kindle system, has the lion's share of the eBook market.

And that's just the tip of the electronic iceberg, the part we can easily see. But there's much more to it. Not only are 164 million customers *buying* their books on Amazon, but millions more are using Amazon's catalog and customer reviews to inform their buying choices elsewhere. That's why Amazon should be ground zero for your promotional efforts. The e-tailer provides free worldwide exposure—exposure to *those readers most likely to buy your book.* Simply having your book properly listed for sale on Amazon can spur demand for it everywhere. Whether you're a famous author or an unknown, Amazon is essential because it has a critical mass of buyers using its search engine, recommendations and reader reviews.

Amazon's 'Long Tail'

Amazon does a good job selling the blockbusters, but anyone can do that. The interesting part is how Amazon can build and focus demand for niche books, those with a widely dispersed audience that can't be targeted effectively with traditional marketing. These are the books readers often can't find in their local bookstore, or even the library—but they're easy to find online. One-quarter of Amazon's book sales come from obscure books that aren't stocked in a Barnes & Noble superstore stocking 100,000 titles. And the percentage of these "long tail" sales grows every year.

Everyone knows about Amazon's discounts and free shipping deals, but its biggest draw is the vast selection, which enables readers to find exactly what they want, says Chris Anderson, author of the business bestseller *The Long Tail*:

> "It's not enough that things be available, you need to be able to find them. The big problem with brick-and-mortar stores is that all shoppers experience the same store. But the problem of 'findability' is solved when you go online. You have searching, recommendations, and all sorts of narrow taxonomies—things can be in multiple categories at the same time."

Amazon's "infinite bookshelves" are revolutionizing the book business. For 50 years, publishers have been chasing blockbusters—the bestseller hits. They had to, because with limited shelf space, bookstores had to focus on the stuff that was a sure seller. Today, chasing blockbusters is obsolete. The niche books are the ones people care about most, and the ones Amazon is most effective in recommending, says Greg Greeley, Amazon's vice president for media products: "The Web site is designed to help customers find books they didn't know existed."

Book momentum is a self-fulfilling prophecy, especially on Amazon. The more people who buy your book, the easier it becomes for the next reader to discover it. When Amazon notices your book is selling, it automatically displays your book higher in its search results and higher in its category lists. And most importantly, Amazon starts plugging your book into book recommendations on its Web site and in e-mails to customers.

Book recommendations are Amazon's biggest sales engine after keyword searches. Two-thirds of book buyers are returning customers, many of them acting on automated recommendations for books popular with customers with similar buying histories.

Because they are personalized, Amazon's book recommendations are better than traditional advertising—more effective than a highway billboard visible to everyone in town. And as long as your book keeps selling, Amazon continues recommending it month after month, year after year, to its likely audience. No longer are books sentenced to the bargain bin three months after publication. Online word of mouth can keep your book alive as long as it satisfies readers.

Personalized Bookstores

Each Amazon customer sees a unique store. The layout is personalized, based on which books the customer previously viewed or purchased. Each customer has a recommendations list, based on which books are bought most frequently by other customers with similar buying histories.

If you have an Amazon account, you can view your recommendations here:

www.amazon.com/gp/yourstore

Because you're an author, understanding Amazon's recommendation system is valuable. Let's imagine you've written the book *How to Grow Organic Strawberries*. It turns out that one of every 15 Amazon customers who buys your book also purchased an earlier book, *Healthy Eating With Organic Fruit*. Realizing this, Amazon starts recommending your book to customers who bought the earlier book but haven't yet bought yours. Why? Amazon knows the odds are good that once these readers discover your book they'll buy it, too. Everyone wins: The buyer finds what they want, and Amazon makes more money.

Buyers see book recommendations in several places:

- At your personalized store, www.amazon.com/yourstore.

- In personalized e-mails, recommending new books (and other merchandise) in categories you typically shop.

- In Amazon's "Frequently Bought Together" list. On Amazon's product page below the "Book Description" you'll often find this list of items most often purchased in combination.

- In a book's "Also Bought" list. Every book's detail page on Amazon includes one or two additional books (or other items) most often purchased with the book featured on the page. These titles appear under the heading "Customers Who Bought This Item Also Bought."

- When their friends purchase a book. Your friends have the option upon making a purchase on Amazon to "share" the information with their friends via a handy message, ready to be posted on Facebook or other social media sites, or they can send an e-mail recommending it to specific people you designate. In fact, they need only add the book to their wish list to do so.

Book Description

Release date: **February 26, 2013** | Series: **The Married Life Series**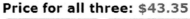

Featuring the headline-grabbing, Eisner Award-nominated, and sold-out wedding of Kevin k
Archie's most popular character in years, *Archie: The Married Life Book 3* explores Archie Ar
⌄ Show more

Frequently Bought Together

 + +

Price for all three: $43.35

[Add all three to Cart] [Add all three to Wish List]

Show availability and shipping details

☑ **This item:** Archie: The Married Life Book 3 (The Married Life Series) by Paul Kupperberg Paperback $13.97

☑ Archie: The Married Life Book 2 by Paul Kupperberg Paperback $14.69

☑ Archie: The Married Life Book 1 by Michael Uslan Paperback $14.69

Customers Who Bought This Item Also Bought

| Archie: The Married Life Book 2 $14.69 | Archie: The Married Life Book 1 $14.69 | The Archie Wedding: Archie in Will You ... $11.58 | Archie: The Married Book 4 (The Married Series) |

Above: the wisdom of crowds and book recommendations.

Amazon's recommendations aren't just a computer talking, it's the collective judgment of millions of people acting independently in their own self-interest. Amazon is the biggest and most effective word-of-mouth generator for books because it measures not what people *say*, but what they *do*. People don't always recommend their favorite current book to each of their friends and acquaintances. But Amazon factors each buying decision into its recommendations for like-minded customers.

Just as a well-programmed computer can defeat a human master chess player, automated recommendations can suggest just the right book, including books that would never occur to a brilliant bookstore clerk, says Amazon chief executive Jeff Bezos:

> "I remember one of the first times this struck me. The main book on the page was about Zen. There were other suggestions for Zen books, but in the middle of those was a [recommended] book on 'How to have a clutter-free desk.'

> That's not something that a human editor would ever pick. But statistically, the people who were interested in the Zen books also wanted clutter-free desks. The computer is blind to the fact that these things are dissimilar in some way to humans. It looks right through that and says, 'Yes, try this.' And it works."

Bubbling to the Top

The more your book sells on Amazon, the more frequently it's shown and recommended. Books that sell well on Amazon appear higher in search results and category lists. And unlike, say, the *New York Times' Sunday Book Review,* which has a generic bestseller list, Amazon has literally hundreds of bestseller lists for every niche of fiction and nonfiction. This provides plenty of opportunities for your book to stand out for its audience.

Let's imagine your book *How to Grow Organic Strawberries* outsells a competing title, *The Complete Moron's Guide to Growing Organic Strawberries.* When Amazon customers search for the keyword "strawberries," your book will appear on top—customers will see it first, and notice it before the competition.

More benefits result from your Amazon sales: Your book moves up in category lists, providing another way for potential readers to discover it. For example, your title on organic strawberries would appear in this Amazon subcategory:

Home & Garden > Gardening & Horticulture >Techniques > Organic

This subcategory list is like a bestseller list for your niche. Amazon has dozens of top-level categories (like "Arts & Photography" and "Business & Investing" divided into dozens more subcategories. Unlike general bestseller lists compiled by the *New York Times* or *USA Today,* Amazon's subcategory lists show what people care about at the niche level, where passions run deepest.

Amazon's subcategories are discrete enough that just a few sales can push your title near the top, exposing your book to more people who care about that topic. In our example subcategory, "Home & Garden > ... Organic," your book could claim one of the top three spots with only a few sales per week on Amazon.

Once you've bubbled up to the top of your subcategory, you're firmly inside the positive feedback loop. Amazon acts as a huge funnel, sending thousands of readers to your book. That's why some authors encourage their friends, website visitors, Facebook friends and everyone else to buy their book from Amazon. Even though an author could perhaps make a bigger short-term profit by selling their book directly, savvy authors know that each Amazon sale boosts their exposure, prompting more sales over the long term.

"Simply put, the more customers you send to Amazon who buy your book, the more visible it will be on Amazon, and the more books Amazon will sell for you," says Morris Rosenthal, publisher of Foner Books.

If your book continues selling for six months or so, Amazon can assign it to more categories, making it even more likely browsers will find you after browsing in related categories. Books that sell moderately well eventually can be assigned to 12 or more categories, the same exposure as your book being shelved in a dozen different sections of a bookstore—the world's biggest bookstore.

To see your book's subcategory assignments on Amazon, find the section on your book's detail page headed "Look for similar items by category." Clicking on those links takes you to a list of the subcategory's bestsellers.

Look for Similar Items by Category

Books > Children's Books > Humor

Books > Children's Books > Science Fiction & Fantasy > Fantasy & Magic

Books > Children's Books > Social Situations > Family Life

Books > Children's Books > Social Situations > Friendship

Books > Children's Books > Social Situations > School

Books > Teens > Science Fiction & Fantasy > Fantasy

Above: A popular book like Harry Potter can extend its footprint into several book subcategories, extending its exposure on Amazon.com

Recommendation Effectiveness

Some recommendations carry more weight than others. Online recommendations are more effective with certain categories of books and price points, according to people who've studied this closely. For example, recommendations for medical texts tended to be most effective—nearly 5.7 percent of them resulted in a purchase, almost double the average rate, according to a study by HP Labs and two universities, who reviewed millions of book purchases resulting from online recommendations. The researchers attributed this to the higher median price of medical books and technical books in general. A higher book price increased the chance that recommendations would be consulted and accepted.

Recommendations were "moderately" effective for certain religious categories: 4.3 percent for Christian living and theology, and 4.8 percent for Bibles. By contrast, books not connected with organized religions had lower recommendation effectiveness, including New Age (2.5 percent) and occult (2.2 percent).

Recommendations for fiction books were usually the least effective, with only about 2 percent resulting in purchases. Recommendations for nonfiction books dealing with personal and leisure pursuits were slightly more effective, resulting in purchases about 3 percent of the time.

Figure 1.1

Recommendation effectiveness by category

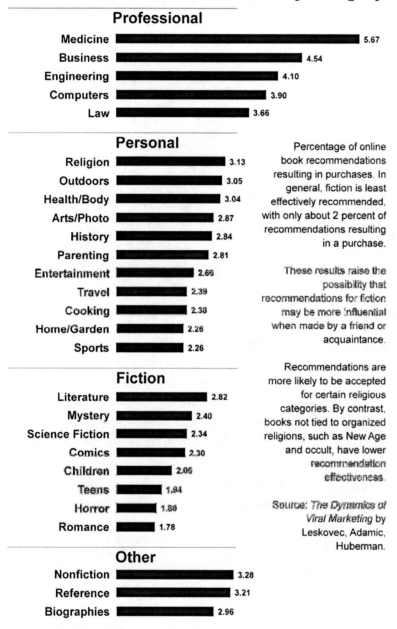

Professional

Medicine	5.67
Business	4.54
Engineering	4.10
Computers	3.90
Law	3.66

Personal

Religion	3.13
Outdoors	3.05
Health/Body	3.04
Arts/Photo	2.87
History	2.84
Parenting	2.81
Entertainment	2.66
Travel	2.39
Cooking	2.38
Home/Garden	2.26
Sports	2.26

Fiction

Literature	2.82
Mystery	2.40
Science Fiction	2.34
Comics	2.30
Children	2.06
Teens	1.94
Horror	1.80
Romance	1.78

Other

Nonfiction	3.28
Reference	3.21
Biographies	2.96

Percentage of online book recommendations resulting in purchases. In general, fiction is least effectively recommended, with only about 2 percent of recommendations resulting in a purchase.

These results raise the possibility that recommendations for fiction may be more influential when made by a friend or acquaintance.

Recommendations are more likely to be accepted for certain religious categories. By contrast, books not tied to organized religions, such as New Age and occult, have lower recommendation effectiveness.

Source: *The Dynamics of Viral Marketing* by Leskovec, Adamic, Huberman.

Figure 1.2

Extremes in book recommendation networks

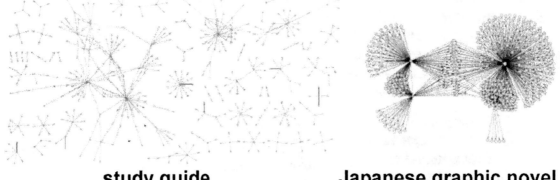

study guide   **Japanese graphic novel**

Above: An illustration of recommendation networks for two very different books. The left shows how recommendations for a study guide were ineffective and ignored by consumers. On the right, recommendations for a graphic novel were effective, resulting in frequent purchases.

The book on the left is the study guide *First Aid for the USMLE Step 1*. The book on the right is *Oh My Goddess!: Mara Strikes Back*. Recommendations for this graphic novel prompted bursts of connected sales represented visually by the linked patterns. The opportunities for networking are vast: Japanese comics have a wide following in the United States, are popular with children and adults, and are vigorously supported by online communities. By contrast, suggestions for study guides usually originate outside online communities, from an instructor or employer. Choice is restricted, online connections are sparse, and no word of mouth occurs. For a variety of reasons, readers are rarely passionate about textbooks.

Generally, though, fiction recommendations are least effective of any book category, resulting in purchases only 2 percent of the time, while recommendations for expensive medical books are most effective.

Illustration from The Dynamics of Viral Marketing

by Leskovec, Adamic, Huberman.

In the cases of fiction or religious books, recommendations from family members or personal friends were much more effective than online recommendations, the researchers concluded.

Some book categories, such as gardening, have different recommendation effectiveness depending on how specialized the text and how widely the topic is supported by online communities. For example, books on vegetable or tomato growing had only average recommendation effectiveness. However, recommendations of books on orchid cultivation had double the recommendation acceptance because the subject was narrower.

Repeated recommendations produce sales, but only to a point. Customers are more likely to buy a book if they receive the same recommendation twice. After that, customers tend to ignore recommendations.

The study is available in its entirety here:

www.hpl.hp.com/research/idl/papers/viral/viral.pdf

Amazon Best Seller Rank

As your sales on Amazon increase, you'll see a corresponding move in your title's "Amazon Best Sellers Rank," sometimes called "Amazon Sales Rank."

Amazon's rankings show how each book is selling compared to every other title in the catalog of nearly 4 million. Updated hourly, the system assigns a unique rank to each book relative to each other title's sales—the top-selling book is ranked 1, and the slowest-selling book is ranked over 9,000,000.

The closer you get to 1, the more often your book appears in Amazon recommendations. For this reason, many entrepreneurial authors concentrate on driving as many sales as possible to Amazon during a book's launch. Enlarging your book's footprint on Amazon can pay dividends for years to come.

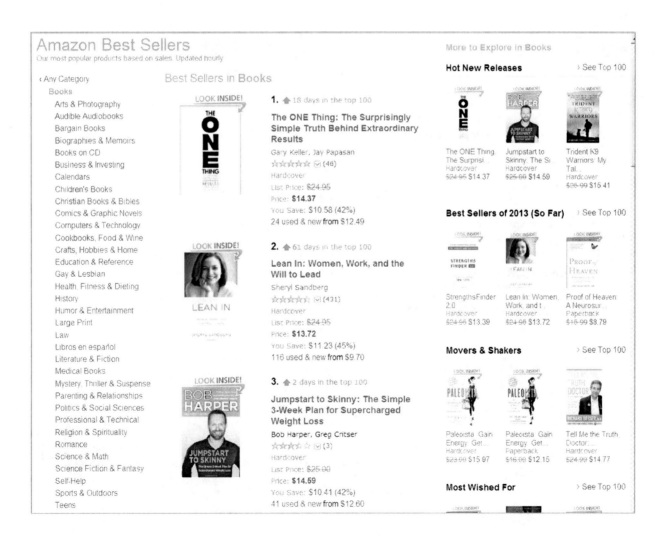

Your book's Amazon Sales Rank is public evidence of how successful your book is. Many booksellers, publishers, and agents pay close attention to Amazon ranks. So if you manage to pump up the sales rank of your book, it can prompt brick-and-mortar stores to order more copies.

Amazon has bestseller lists for every category, paperback and Kindle, fiction and nonfiction, and virtually every subcategory.

You can explore Amazon's bestseller lists by starting at the home page:

www.amazon.com/Best-Sellers/zgbs

Amazon's Author Central

Amazon produces a ton of sales because it empowers customers to easily find what they're looking for at good prices. Similarly, Amazon empowers authors to help refine how their work is presented on the marketplace.

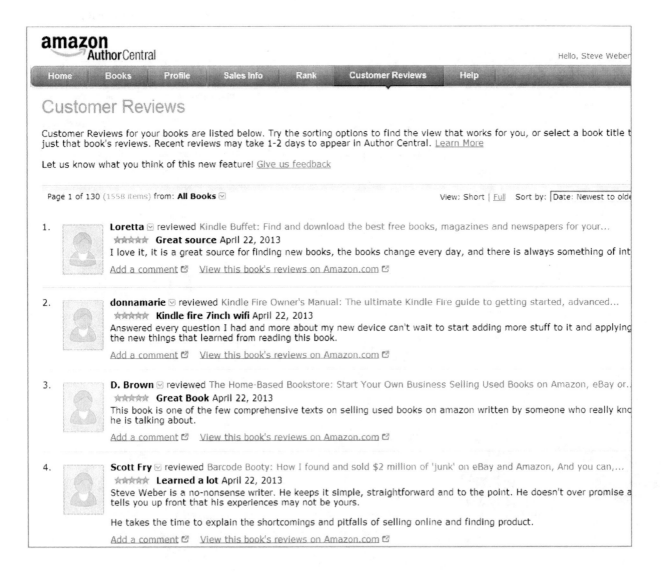

Above: This tab of Author Central shows the most recent customer reviews for an author's books. Author Central is Amazon's service that allows authors to accomplish several tasks from a central location: https://authorcentral.amazon.com/

The advent of Author Central a few years ago was a great blessing for authors. Previously, authors had little control over how their books were presented on Amazon.com. Replacing a missing cover image or correcting a mistake in a book description could often lead to weeks of frustration because Amazon's book cataloging department was notoriously hard to communicate with. Now authors can edit the information themselves, and corrections are posted promptly.

Author Central also enables authors to publish a profile page on Amazon and a bibliography enabling readers to learn about your complete body of work.

There is space for blog posts and Twitter content in a column to the right of your biography.

In addition to the wealth of information it provides to your readers, Author Central contains a treasure trove of information displayed only to authors. This includes sales figures for your books from Neilsen Bookscan, which is a nice perk considering that publishers pay Neilsen at least $799 for access to all its reports. And Author Central provides easy access to Amazon's support staff who help authors manage these details.

Your Author Page is similar in appearance to other pages on Amazon. In the upper left corner of the page, under the standard Amazon Shopping and Search toolbar, your name appears in large type. Beneath your name is space for photos and a biography.

In this column you will also see book recommendations from Amazon, under the heading "Customers Also Bought Items By."

Below your biography, Amazon lists all of your available books in each format.

Next is a section for "Customer Discussions." If an Amazon customer posts a question or a reply concerning one of your books, it will appear here and, simultaneously, on your book's page at Amazon.com. It's one more avenue to provide new information to people interested in you or your literary products, and another reason to monitor your profile closely—if someone poses a question for you, they won't be impressed if you don't reply promptly. You can subscribe to e-mail updates of each new post.

On the following page: the Author Central page for Danielle Steel,

http://www.amazon.com/Danielle-Steel/e/B000APK2GC

From the Author |

From Wikipedia

Danielle Steel has been hailed as one of the world's most popular authors, with over 590 million copies of her novels sold. Her many international bestsellers include 44 Charles Street, Legacy, Family Ties, Big Girl, Southern Lights, Matters of the Heart, One Day at a Time, and other highly acclaimed novels. She is also the author of His Bright Light, the story of her son Nick Traina's life and death.

Danielle Steel on Kindle

Since 1981, Danielle Steel has been a permanent fixture on *The New York Times* hardcover and paperback bestseller lists. And now, her books are available on Kindle. Download the latest, *One Day at a Time*, today.

> See all Steel on Kindle

Latest Tweet

daniellesteel
Publisher's Weekly just gave my upcoming novel "Until the End of Time" a great review. Yay! I hope you will like it too. On stands 1/29.
9 days ago via web twitter

Biography

In 1989, Danielle Steel was listed in the Guinness Book of World Records for having at least one of her books on the Times bestseller list for 381 consecutive weeks. But Guinness was premature. The fact is that one or more of Ms. Steel's novels have been on the *New York Times* bestseller list for over 390 consecutive weeks.

Books by Danielle Steel

Showing 1 - 12 of 269 Results   Sort by [New and Popular ▾]

All Formats   Kindle Edition   Paperback   Hardcover   Audible Audio Edition   See more ⌄

The Sins of the Mother: A Novel by Danielle Steel (Oct 30, 2012)
★★★★☆ (302 customer reviews)

Formats	Price	New	Used	Collectible
Hardcover Order in the next 5 hours to get it by Tuesday, Jan 15.	~~$28.00~~ $15.61 *Prime*	$9.54	$7.18	$28.00
Kindle Edition Auto-delivered wirelessly	$13.99			

Other Formats: Audible Audio Edition; Paperback; Audio CD

Sell this back for an Amazon.com Gift Card

Until the End of Time: A Novel by Danielle Steel (Jan 29, 2013)

Formats	Price	New	Used
Hardcover Available for Pre-order. This item will be released on January 29, 2013. Pre-order Price Guarantee. See Details	~~$28.00~~ $18.48 *Prime*		
Kindle Edition Available for Pre-order. This item will be released on January 29, 2013.	$13.99		

Other Formats: Audible Audio Edition; Paperback; Audio CD

Legacy: A Novel by Danielle Steel (Sep 28, 2010)
★★★★☆ (93 customer reviews)

Formats	Price	New	Used
Hardcover Order in the next 5 hours to get it by Tuesday, Jan 15.	~~$28.00~~ $11.20 *Prime*	$3.13	$2.08
Kindle Edition Auto-delivered wirelessly	$7.99		

Other Formats: Audible Audio Edition; Paperback; Mass Market Paperback; Audio CD

⟨ Previous Page   1 2 3 ... 23   Next Page ⟩

> See search results for author "Danielle Steel" in Books

Customers Also Bought Items By

Nora Roberts   Janet Evanovich

Debbie Macomber   E. L. James

James Patterson   Marshall Karp

Nicholas Sparks   David Baldacci

John Grisham   Barbara Taylor...

Sandra Brown   Michael Connelly

Fern Michaels   Jackie Collins

Mary Higgins Clark   Stuart Woods

Amazon Author Rank beta (What's this?)

#64 Overall (See top 100 authors)

#10 in Kindle eBooks > Fiction > **Contemporary Fiction**
#14 in Books > Literature & Fiction > **Genre Fiction**
#14 in Books > Romance > **Contemporary**
#16 in Kindle eBooks > Fiction > Romance > **Contemporary**
#20 in Books > **Romance**

Are You an Author?

Help us improve our Author Pages by updating your bibliography and submitting a new or current image and biography.

> Learn how to submit changes at Author Central

Customer Discussions

Danielle Steel forum

Discussion	Replies	Latest Post
⊞ My Favorite	6	Jan 4, 2012

> See all discussions...   > Start a new discussion

Setting up Your Author Central Account

Here's how to set up your Author Central account:

1. Visit **https://authorcentral.amazon.com** and click "Join Now." Enter your e-mail address and password and click "Sign in." If you have an Amazon.com account, sign in with the e-mail address and password you use on that account.

2. Read the Author Central's Terms and Conditions, and then click "Agree" to accept them.

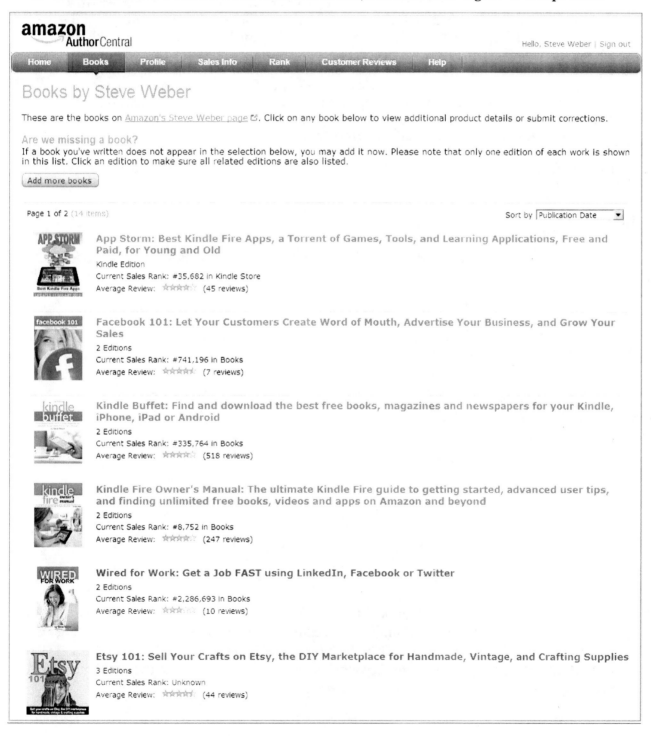

3. Enter the name your books are written under. A list of possible book matches appears.

4. Select any one of your books. If your book is not in the list, you can search for it by title or ISBN. Selecting the book creates the account.

5. Amazon will send you a confirmation e-mail with a link that you will need to click to confirm your e-mail address and identity. In some cases, they may need to contact your publishers to verify your association with the book. If you've signed in with a different e-mail address than the one your publisher is familiar with, contact them with this information so they can quickly approve you.

6. While you're waiting for approval, you still can use some of Author Central's features. For example, you can add or edit a photo or biography. Amazon will not publish the content until verification is complete. Other updates, such as blogging and making changes to the books listed in your bibliography, are not available until you're confirmed.

Once you are confirmed and you follow the link from the confirmation e-mail, you will see a message like this when you sign into Author Central.

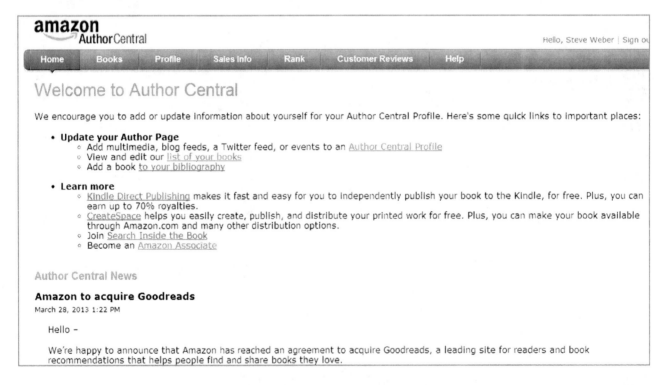

Biography: Click on the words "add biography" to tell readers who you are, what you enjoy writing, and more. Amazon will ask you to include a minimum of 20 characters in plain text only. Before filling out this section of the page, take some time to look at the biographies of other authors you admire and view the sample biography Amazon provides. This is your chance to present yourself to the world on one of the world's biggest marketplaces—make it good!

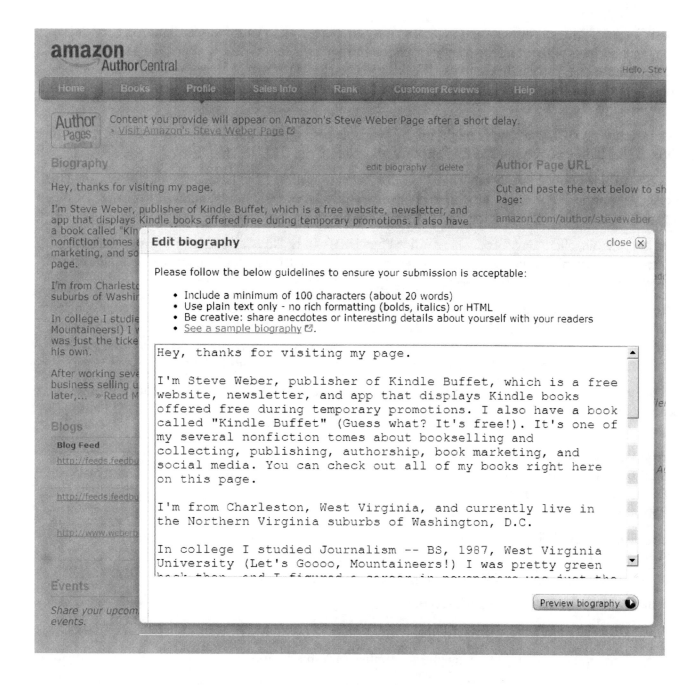

Blogs: Author Central allows you to link to a blog you've created elsewhere. They support any version of an RSS and Atom blog feed. You need only click "add blog" and then specify the web address of your blog *feed* in the window that appears. Only blog posts that have been created from this point on will appear on your Author Page; if you want previous blog posts to appear there, you must go back to your blog and re-post them on your blog.

Events: You may share your upcoming tour dates, bookstore appearances, speaking engagements, and any other promotional event on your Author Central page. Click on "add an event" and then complete the form that appears to Create Event. You will be asked to add a description of the event, specify where by adding a venue, and specify which of your books the event pertains to. Add an event date and start time, click "save event" and you are finished.

Author Page URL: An Author Page URL is an easy-to-share link to your page on Amazon.com. It is a cleaner web address without all the numbers, codes and symbols that typically appear in a web address. Once you create one, you can begin to use it in all your marketing efforts. You may use letters, numbers, dashes, periods and underscores, but no spaces, and no other special characters. You may choose to use a maximum of 30 characters.

Occasionally a URL you specify might not be available because it might be already assigned to another author. If this happens, you need to find another variation of the URL and request it.

On the Author Central Profile tab, click "add link" next to Author Page URL. Type in your chosen URL, typically your name but it can be anything; choose carefully, as you will not be allowed to change it! When you type it in, Amazon will check for the URL's availability.

If it is available, click "Save" and your Author Page URL will be "live" and able to be used in about 30 minutes. If unavailable, Amazon will suggest a variation of the URL which you may accept or choose to create your own. Then repeat the process of saving.

Photos: Amazon allows you to share up to eight photos of yourself on your Author Profile page. Click on "Add Photo." Be sure to only post photos that you either own or have the right to post; you will be asked to confirm this before you are able to upload them. Amazon allows only JPEG photos (no GIFs, PNGs or other formats). They must be between 300 and 2,500 pixels and be no larger than 4 MB.

To upload photos, click on the Choose File button; this opens a window that allows you to browse and choose a photo from a folder on your computer. Choose your photo and then click the Upload Photo button.

Videos: You may share videos that pertain to your book, such as video interviews, videos of book signings, or videos with your readers. Any video you upload to your Author Profile page should be specific to a feature of your book(s), or your experience as an author. As with photos, you must confirm that you own the video or have permission to display it on Amazon.

The reason Amazon allows you to put videos on your Profile Page is to encourage people to buy your book on Amazon. Therefore, suggesting an alternative—like buying your book from Barnes & Noble—is a no-no. You're also prohibited from discussing the price or ordering information for your book.

Amazon also discourages videos which contain:

- Obscene or otherwise distasteful content, profanity or what they term as "spiteful remarks."

- Personal information such as phone numbers or e-mail address

- Other people's material (this content should be about you, and written by you.)

- Solicitations for positive reviews

- Spoilers. Don't reveal your book's crucial plot elements

- Anything else that is in violation of Amazon's Content Guidelines. See http://www.amazon.com/gp/help/customer/display.html?nodeId=15015801

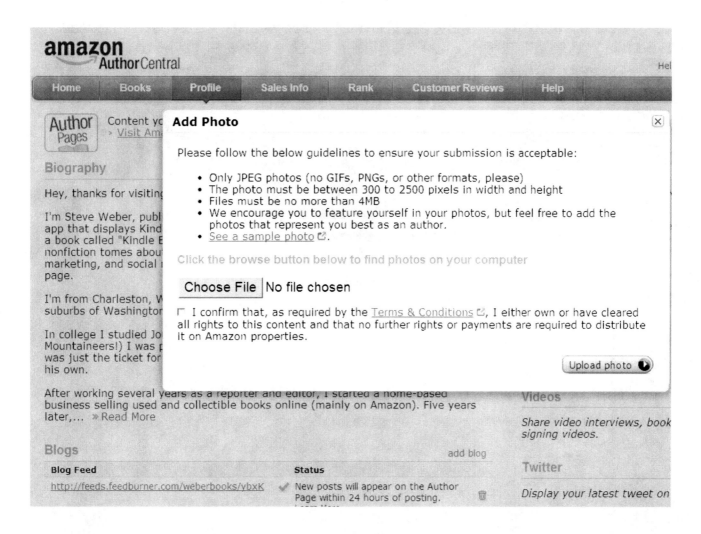

You may add up to eight videos as long as they don't exceed 10 minutes in length and 500 MB in size. Acceptable formats are avi, wmv, flv, mov, or mpg.

To upload a video from the Author Central Profile page, click "Add Video." This opens a window that allows you to choose a file from your computer. Amazon may take up to 24 hours to process the upload of your video(s). When processing is finished, you'll receive an e-mail asking you to review and approve the video before it's made available to customers.

Twitter: Similar to your blog feed, if you use Twitter, you can automatically add your tweets to your Amazon profile. To display your latest tweet, click on "Add Account."Enter your Twitter username and click "Save." Only your most recent tweet will appear on your Amazon profile.

Review your "Books" tab: When you click on the "Books" Tab from your Profile page in Author Central, you'll arrive at a page entitled "Books by [Author Name]," otherwise known as your Bibliography. The information you enter here will be shown to Amazon shoppers who click on your author name at various places on Amazon.com. Ensure the list of books is complete, listing all available editions of your work.

Adding books to your Bibliography: To add more of your books to the list, click on the tab "Add More Books."

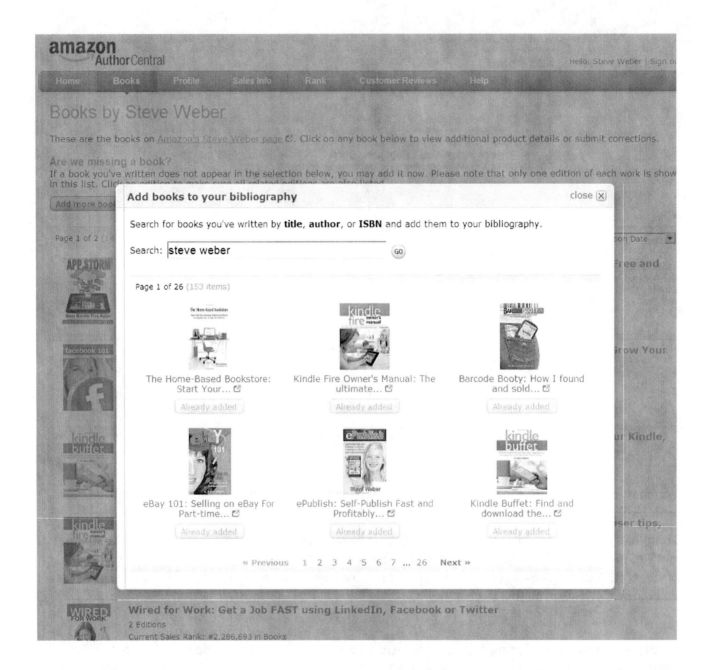

In the window that appears, you may search Amazon for your books by Title, Author, or ISBN. Choose your book from among the search results, and click on the "This is my Book" button. If your name appears as the author of the work, you will be asked to verify that this is the correct book. Click "This is Me" to add it to your Bibliography.

If you are not listed as the author of the book you are trying to add—for example, if you are a contributor rather than the primary author—you may contact Amazon and request to have your name added to the book. Amazon's staff will verify the information with the publisher before you'll be able to add the book to your Bibliography.

When one of your books appears on the "Books" tab, you may click on the title of the book to manage the book's description and other details, submit corrections, and specify other available editions.

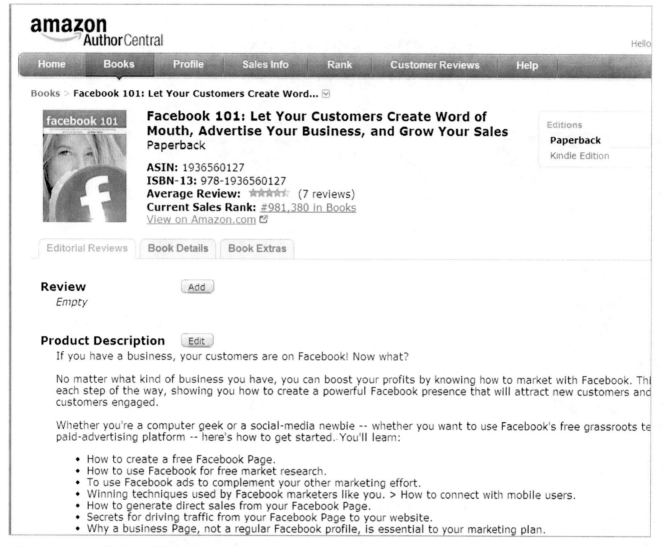

Above: An individual book page at Author Central.

At the top left of the page is an image of your book cover (assuming Amazon has one available). Next to the image is the title, edition, the ASIN or ISBN numbers, the number of customer reviews, an average of the customer reviews represented by an image of one to five gold stars, and its current Amazon Best Sellers Rank.

ISBNs and ASINs. In case you're unfamiliar with these numbers, this is a good place to define ASINs and ISBNs, which are specified in the "Product Details" section of product pages at Amazon.com. Paperback and hardcover books usually have a 13-digit ISBN, or International Standard Book Number.

Amazon products are identified with a unique 10-digit ASIN, or Amazon Standard Item Number.

Next are three tabs where you can click to add more information about your book—Editorial Reviews, Book Details, and Book Extras.

If you're represented by a publishing company, it's important to coordinate your changes to your Editorial Reviews, Book Details, and Book Extras tabs. Once you've entered or edited information in these tabs, your publisher will not be able to make further changes to the same section.

Editorial Reviews Tab: There are several sections you can complete under the Editorial Reviews Tab.

Add an Editorial Review: Do you have a favorite review you'd like to share with customers—perhaps a review from a newspaper or blog? Click on the Add button and type or paste it into the "Add Review screen." Be sure to read the guidelines at the top of the screen, which explain that reviews should contain only one or two sentences totaling fewer than 600 characters.

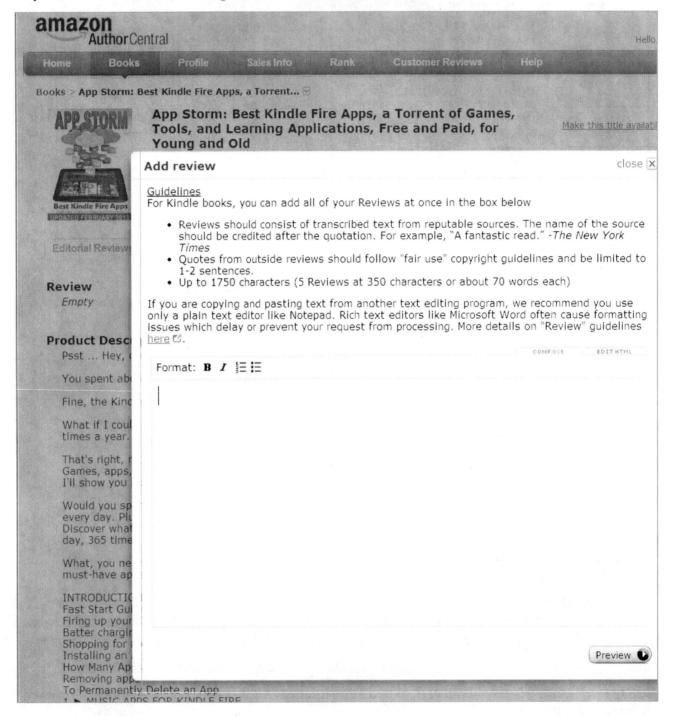

Reviews should be transcribed from a "reputable source" and that source should be credited for the quotation. When you are finished adding the review, click Preview and, when satisfied with it, click Save Changes.

After the new information is published to your book's product page, which may take a few days, you can edit the wording at any point in the future by visiting the same tab.

More suggestions and guidelines are available in Amazon's Help Pages:

https://authorcentral.amazon.com/gp/help?ie=UTF8&topicID=200649600

Product Description: Here is where you have a chance to explain to readers what your book is about and why they should read it. This can make or break the sale, so it's important to have a compelling pitch here. Your Product Description should begin with an objective summary of the book, specify the genre, and explain why your book is different.

The description can have a maximum of 2,400 characters, which is approximately 480 words.

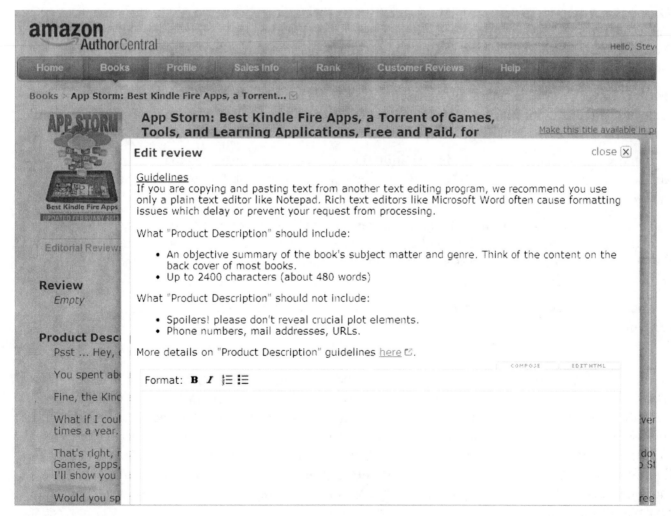

Above: the "Add a review" screen at Author Central.

Enter your Description: Click on the "Edit" button next to the Product Description. You will be taken to a screen with a box that you may type or paste details into. When you are finished adding the review, click "Preview" and, after you're satisfied with it, click "Save Changes."

From the Author: You can include a personal message about your book. You might include an anecdote explaining your inspiration for writing the book, or how it fits in with your other books. This section may be up to 8,000 characters long, or about 1,600 words.

When you are finished adding the details, click "Preview" and, when satisfied with it, click "Save Changes."

From the Inside Flap and From the Back Cover: As the title of these sections suggests, this is where you add your book's inside and back cover copy. To do so, click on the "Add" button next to the words "Inside Flap" or "From the Back Cover."

The content of the inside flap or back cover copy should be transcribed exactly as is, without changes. It may be up to 8,000 characters, or 1600 words. When you are finished adding the details, click "Preview" and, when satisfied with it, click "Save Changes."

About the Author: To add information about you as the author, click on "Add."In the screen that comes up, type or paste the same (or similar) information that appears in your biography on your Author Profile page. This section can accommodate up to 2000 characters (or about 400 words.) When you are finished adding the details, click "Preview" and, when satisfied with it, click "Save Changes."

Book Details Tab: Click on the "Book Details" Tab at the top of the page. Under this tab you will see basic information about your book, including the name of your publisher, your book's publication date, language and the number of pages.

If you'd like to change any of the information that you see on this page, you may submit a form to Amazon with suggested changes. They will research your suggestion and if they agree with the changes, they will go ahead and change the record.

To suggest changes, click on the link for "Suggest product information updates."Make changes to the form that is provided. At the bottom of the page you can check one of the boxes under the heading "I Know I'm Correct Because..." to assist Amazon in verifying that your changes are indeed correct. Here you also have the opportunity to submit photos to help them verify your change.

Then, click "Preview Your Updates" at the bottom of the page. Amazon will then begin the process of verifying that your changes are correct before publishing them on this page.

Book Extras Tab: Here's an avenue for providing yet more information about your books using the "Book Extras" tab and Shelfari.com. Shelfari, owned by Amazon, is a community-powered encyclopedia for book lovers. People can join the site for free and create a virtual bookshelf, discover new books, and connect with friends. It's a way for people to suggest books to their friends or anyone, really. Many use it to keep track of lists of books they have read, and when. When they begin reading a book, they add it to their Shelfari shelf. When they finish reading it, they can record the date they finished, and give it a thorough review. Avid readers will use Shelfari as yet one more way to search for book suggestions, and may pay attention to the reviews they read there.

The Extras that currently appear under the Book Extras tab are details about your book that have been submitted by people in the Shelfari community. These are different than the reviews that are submitted by people on Amazon. They do not appear on Amazon's review page, but are visible to people who view your book page using Kindle devices and apps. But they can include material you have submitted through Shelfari.

Among the extras you and/or others can submit through Shelfari:

- Synopsis
- Summary
- Characters/People
- Versions of the Book Cover
- Quotes
- Setting and Locations
- First Sentence
- Table of Contents
- Glossary
- Themes and Symbolism
- Series and Lists
- Authors and Contributors
- Awards
- Notes for Parents
- ... and more

The more information out there about your book, the easier it is to attract readers to it, so make these categories work for you by sharing accurate, enticing information.

Currently, Shelfari-submitted details can be accessed by customers through their Kindle and Kindle apps for iPad, iPhone and iPod Touch. On the Kindle device, while reading, a link to Book Extras appears below Customer Reviews. On Kindle for iPhone and Kindle for iPad, while reading, you can select Book Extras by touching the book icon at the bottom of the screen.

To manage details that others may have already posted about your books at Shelfari:

Click on the Book Extras Tab at the top of the page. On the Book Extras tab, there is a link directly to your book's page on Shelfari.com where you can add or edit the information. Because you must be signed into Author Central to access your Book Extras Tab on your Book's page of your Author Profile, and because Shelfari is owned by Amazon, when you log into Shelfari to make changes to the Book Extras details you will receive an author badge—which will identify you, as the book's author, who is making the additions and changes to Shelfari.

Book Extras is edited for accuracy by the community, including you. If you see something that is inaccurate, you can correct it yourself, flag that piece of content as inaccurate or inappropriate, or delete it. All changes to the content are tracked and visible to the entire community. You can delete offensive content—content that is obscene, defamatory, fraudulent, inciting, or criminal in nature—and also report it to feedback@shelfari.com.

To monitor changes to your book's page on Shelfari, click on the box labeled "notify me when this page changes." Whenever someone posts on your book's page you can check its accuracy and respond if necessary.

Spoilers: If a comment is identified as containing a plot spoiler, the notice "Spoiler Alert!" appears. Readers who want to read the spoiler click the down arrow and proceed to the book page on Shelfari to read the full comment.

If you find content that should be identified as a spoiler but isn't, you can mark it as a spoiler, and the alert will appear.

Why Book Extras might not appear: Book Extras appears on a book's Product Detail Page only after several Shelfari comment sections about the book are filled out. This is another good reason to create the content yourself.

Just as with the Books Extras tab, the Shelfari book page has tabs for Readers & Reviews, Discussions, and Editions. You should check these frequently to monitor and participate in these discussions. You may find that other authors and readers who are Shelfari members begin to "follow" your Shelfari account, send e-mails, and otherwise communicate with you as a fellow author or reader. This is fantastic, because anything that builds awareness of your books is a good thing.

If there is no data currently on Shelfari about your books, start creating some. It enables people to find your book and hear more about it, which can only help sales.

Sales Info: Under the Author Central "Sales Info" tab, authors have access to their book's sales data. You can take a look at Sales by Geography, Sales by Week, and Bestsellers Rank History for your books.

The "Sales by Geography" feature reports on your print sales by region. The provider of the data, Nielsen BookScan, reports about 75 percent of retail print book sales in the United States. This includes paper books sold by bookstores and Amazon.com, but it doesn't include Kindle editions or other digital formats.

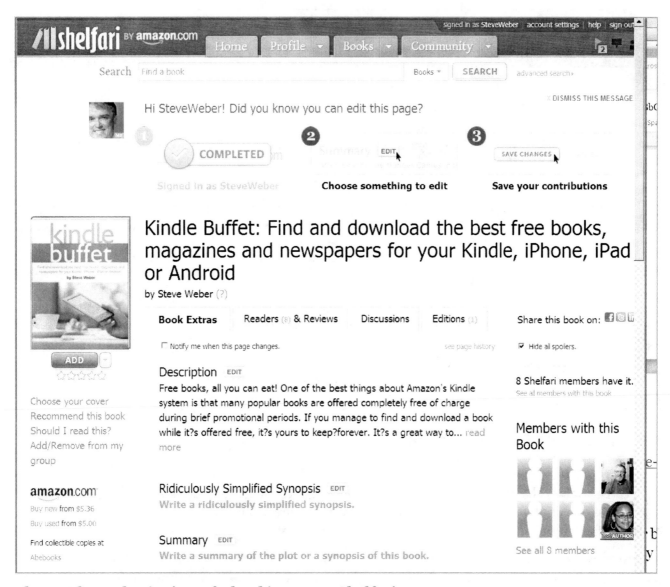

Above: The author's view of a book's page at Shelfari.com.

Geographic info: Hover your cursor over any area of the sales map and you'll see the number of copies of your book that have been sold in that region. Retailers that report these sales include Barnes & Noble, Target and Buy.com. The figures don't include wholesale purchases or sales to libraries. Some large retailers like Wal-Mart and Sam's Club don't report sales figures to Neilsen, either.

You may specify the period of the data you want to review, and sales information can be further broken down to format, such as hardcover sales compared to paperback sales.

Author Rank: Click on the "Amazon Author Rank" tab to see your ranking compared to other authors, based on combined sales of all your books. Like the rankings of individual books, your author rank is updated hourly.

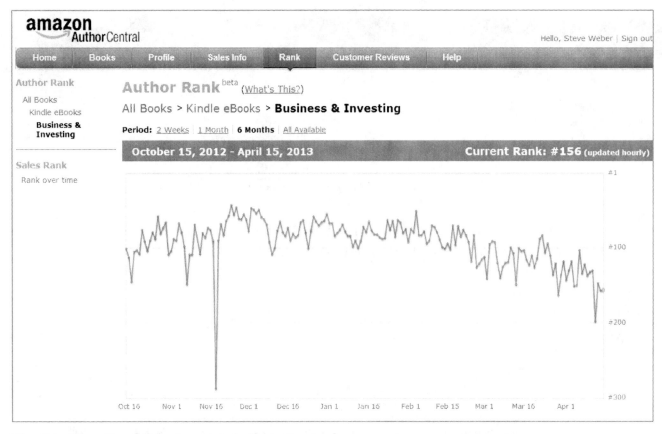

The "Author Rank" feature at Author Central.

You can also filter the rank by clicking on categories listed to the left of the graph, so you can see how you are ranked overall, in Kindle books vs. print books if you are selling both editions, and in the category your books fall within, such as all "Business and Investing" books.

Customer Reviews: Here's a good place to monitor the reviews that Amazon customers write about your books. This Author Central tab provides a central location to see all the reviews, preventing the need for you to visit each book's page on Amazon.com to check for new reviews.

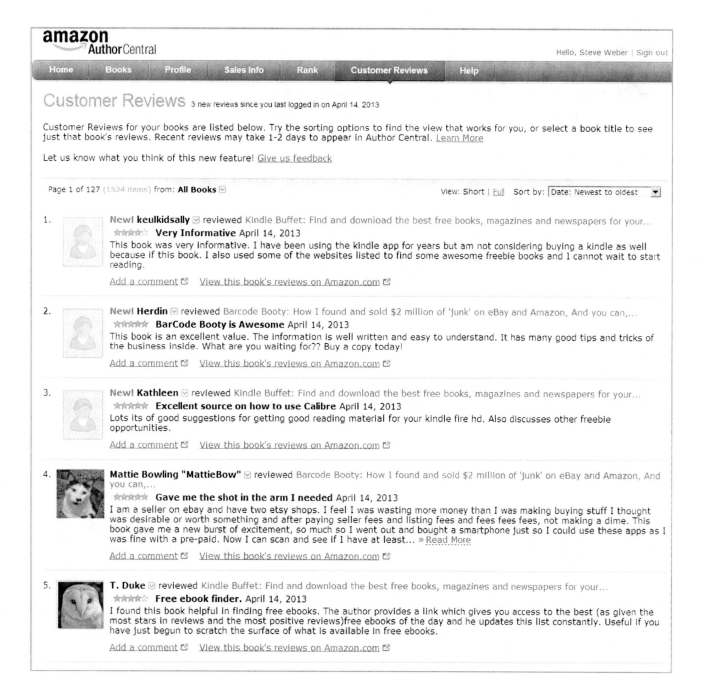

Amazon Sales Rank: One of the favorite pastimes of authors is checking the Amazon Sales Ranks of their books. Sometimes referred to as "Amazon Bestseller Rank," the figure ranges from #1 (for the overall bestselling book) to a number exceeding 8 million for the poorest or slowest-selling book of all.

Amazon ranks each book based on how often it sells relative to every other book in its catalog of some 3.5 million titles.

A book's Amazon Sales Rank appears in the Product Details section of its detail page on Amazon. Sales ranks are recalculated hourly, and can change significantly day to day.

Since Amazon has an estimated 70 percent market share among Internet book retailers, its sales rankings are the best free, publicly available information about the relative sales performance of individual titles. The rankings include new and used books sold by third-party sellers on Amazon's Marketplace platform.

Amazon doesn't publicly discuss its sales figures for individual titles, so it's impossible to correlate the rankings with quantity of sales. However, based on anecdotal reports from various publishers, you can assume that an Amazon sales rank of 5,000 translates into about 25 to 30 sales per day, depending on seasonal factors.

More information about sales ranks: Author Central isn't the only place you can find data concerning Amazon ranks. In the past few years, several free tools have emerged to help authors and publishers monitor the ranks of their books and competing titles.

One of my favorites, Sales Rank Express, is useful for tracking the Amazon Sales Ranks of various books in any of its available formats, such as paperback, hardcover or Kindle. The website provides ranks for each territory where Amazon sells books: United States, Canada, United Kingdom, Spain, France, Italy, Germany, Japan and China. To test-drive Sales Rank Express, visit:

www.salesrankexpress.com

Novel Rank offers a slightly different take on Amazon Sales Ranks, and also estimates the number of units a book sells on Amazon during a given period. Novel Rank also is available as an app for the iPhone. See:

www.novelrank.com

Amazon maintains separate sales rankings for paper books and Kindle books, and another ranking list is dedicated to free Kindle books. You can view the top 100 sellers in each category here:

www.amazon.com/Best-Sellers/zgbs

Getting Book Reviews and Publicity

Keith Donohue had an idea for a book, a story rattling around in his brain for years. But he could never find the time to write it. With a full-time job and a family with three young children, he just kept putting it off.

Then Donohue turned 40, and a short time later came the horrible events of Sept. 11, 2001. He finally realized "It's now or never," and the red-haired Irishman began writing. He wrote on scraps of paper on the subway to work in Washington, D.C., and scribbled during his lunch hour sitting on park benches.

Finally, after several months of rewriting and polishing, the story was finished: *The Stolen Child*, a fantasy inspired by the W.B. Yeats poem and what Donohue knew of the changeling legend.

But the relief of finishing his book gave way to frustration, nearly causing him to give up. It took Donohue two years to find an agent to agree to present the manuscript to publishers. Along the way, he received 10 rejection letters. Finally, Donohue got a call from an agent who'd had the manuscript for a year and misplaced it. Soon Nan Talese of Doubleday took on the book, and it seemed success was at hand.

By 2006, Donohue's book was finally in print. Unfortunately, none of the book critics at big U.S. newspapers and journals were too impressed with *The Stolen Child*. In fact, they completely ignored it; not a single major paper even mentioned it.

But the story wasn't over. A review copy of the book ended up in the hands of Linda Porco, Amazon.com's merchandising director. She passed it among her office mates, and it was unanimous— everyone loved it. So Porco tried something new. She got more copies of the book and mailed them to Amazon's most active customer reviewers. They review books on the site as a hobby, assigning five stars to the books they love, one star to the books they hate, and an essay explaining why.

Within weeks, 13 of these Amazon Top Reviewers posted a rave review. Promptly, *Stolen Child* became Amazon's top-selling fiction book, and reached No. 26 on the *New York Times* extended bestseller list, an unbelievable climb for a novel with no big newspaper or trade reviews. Within a year, the hardcover was in its eighth printing.

All this caused quite a stir in publishing circles, but it didn't surprise the folks who actually buy books. Increasingly, readers turn to online reviews written by peers to find out if a book is worth it. Talese, the publisher, says a traditional function of professional critics—building awareness of a new book—is practically obsolete in the Internet age:

> "We're trying to reach readers. [Professional reviews] have been a way of announcing that a book exists that readers might be interested in, but they are being given less and less room in the newspapers."

Skeptics argue that amateur reviews are meaningless, that they don't possess the same intellectual rigor as reviews from the pros. But when was the last time you ran out and bought a book after seeing it reviewed in a newspaper or magazine? The truth is, many "professional" reviews are simply rehashes of publisher-generated publicity. Most importantly, professional critics usually don't tell readers the one thing they want to know—whether they'll like the book. Readers can get better advice on Amazon. Whatever the amateur reviewers lack in highbrow sensibilities, they make up in credibility and relevancy.

Credibility Through Peers

Successful books have lots of positive reviews on Amazon, and it's no coincidence. It's the positive feedback loop: Good books garner good reviews, which leads to more sales. Good reviews on Amazon are particularly crucial for books by new authors and niche books.

Positive reviews on Amazon boost your sales not only on Amazon, but everywhere people are buying books. What percentage of buyers at brick-and-mortar bookstores actually made their choice by reading Amazon customer reviews? There's no way of knowing exactly, but rest assured it's a substantial and growing number.

Amazon's reviews are effective because they're often written by people who are knowledgeable and passionate about the book and its topic. They're seen as an objective evaluation from someone with no ax to grind. Sure, many inept and biased reviews appear, but savvy shoppers learn how to ignore them.

Getting More Amazon Reviews

Traditional book marketing strategies call for mailing hundreds of review copies to reviewers at magazines and newspapers. But for a new author with a niche book, chasing print reviews can be more of a distraction than a strategy. A better way to launch your campaign is by finding 100 readers in your target audience and *giving them your book*. Ask them to post an honest critique on Amazon. This costs nothing more than mailing review copies to traditional book reviewers, but will likely have a bigger, more immediate impact. Here's where you can begin finding review candidates:

- From Amazon's list of Top Reviewers who regularly post reviews of books similar to yours.

- Amazon users who have reviewed related titles, or books by authors with a writing style similar to yours.

- Acquaintances and colleagues interested in your book's topic.

- Participants in Internet discussion boards and mailing lists relevant to your book.

- Your Facebook friends.

An effective method of getting your book into the hands of lots of reviewers is by sponsoring a book giveaway on a book-oriented site like Goodreads.com (more on this later). The initial readers who enjoy your book will recommend it to friends, and those new readers will recommend it to more people.

Obscurity is the greatest threat to authors, not the cost of giving away some freebies, says Tim O'Reilly, founder of the tech publishing house that bears his name.

One drawback to distributing paperback review copies of your book is that some of them will quickly appear for sale on Amazon Marketplace, even if you stamp "Review Copy, Not For Sale" on the front cover. Although Amazon's policies prohibit the sale of review copies, it still occurs, and of course you'll receive no revenue from those sales. Don't stay awake at night worrying about people selling your review copies. It's part of the cost of doing business for successful authors.

Amazon Top Reviewers

The Stolen Child author Keith Donohue was lucky that Amazon Top Reviewers helped make his book a bestseller; it wasn't part of his plan. But you don't need to depend on luck. Seek out Top Reviewers yourself and ask them to read and review your book. This takes some legwork, but if your book is a good one, it will be well worth the trouble. Reviews from some of Amazon's Top Reviewers can seriously boost the credibility of your book.

Amazon's Top Reviewers are listed here:

www.amazon.com/review/top-reviewers

Top Reviewers have a special badge accompanying their pen names, such as *Top 1000 Reviewer, Top 500 Reviewer, Top 50 Reviewer, Top 10 Reviewer* or *#1 Reviewer*. Having one of these badges displayed among your book's reviews isn't the same thing as an endorsement by Amazon—it's better. It's a vote by a recognized community leader—someone who takes reviewing seriously and has earned a reputation for helpfulness.

Rankings of the Top Reviewers are determined by a point system based on the number of reviews written and the number of positive votes those reviews receive when people click "Yes" in response to "Was this review helpful to you?"

Most Top Reviewers are regular Amazon customers who simply enjoy reading and critiquing lots of books. Many of them review several books per week—sometimes at the invitation of an author or publisher, but usually by just following their personal interests. Despite receiving no payment for their efforts, Amazon Top Reviewers compete furiously to climb the rankings ladder, some of them submitting several reviews each day.

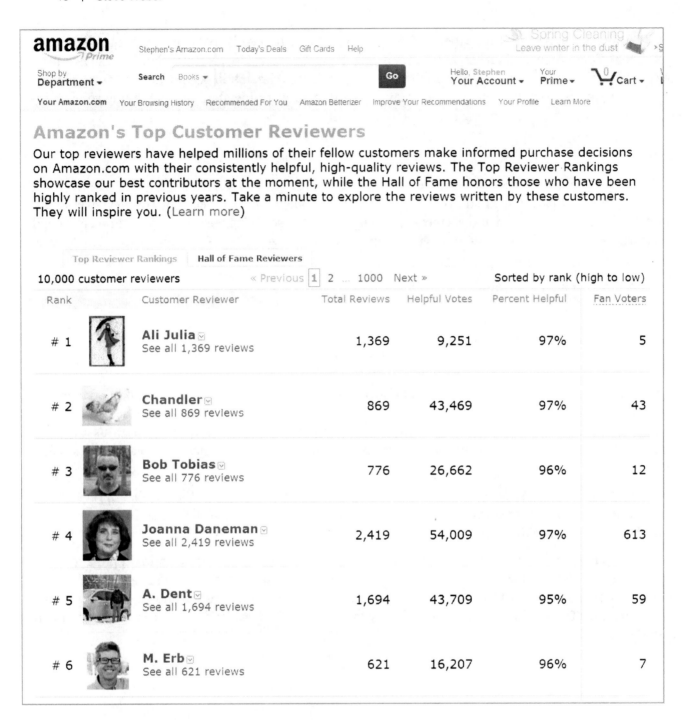

Contacting Top Reviewers

Clicking on a reviewer's pen name takes you to their Amazon profile containing biographical and other information they've posted about themselves. Some reviewer profiles will explain what types of books they prefer. For example, some reviewers stick with fiction; some review only movies or music; some profiles indicate whether the reviewer accepts unsolicited books. And then some provide a postal or e-mail address; some invite communication through their Facebook profile. Some review only paperback copies, while others prefer receiving a Kindle edition.

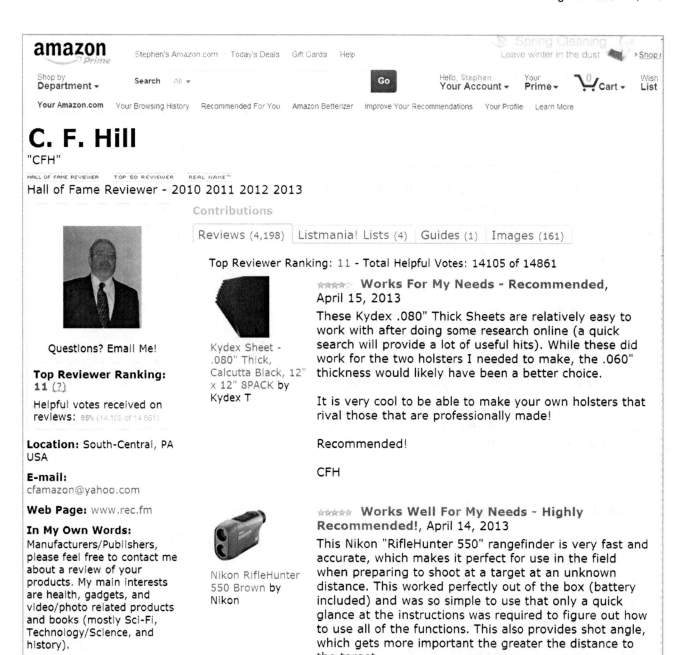

Above: The Amazon profile page for C.F. Hill, a top-ten Amazon reviewer: In the left column, he provides his e-mail and other contact information, and he explains what type of books and gadgets he considers for review.

A soft-sell approach works best when approaching Top Reviewers. Offer a complimentary book in return for their *considering* to review it, no obligation. Most Top Reviewers don't want to commit to a review until they've seen the book. Don't ask reviewers to return the book.

Here's a sample script you might use to approach Amazon Top Reviewers:

Dear John Doe:

I found your name on the list of Amazon Top Reviewers. I've written a book, "How to Grow Organic Strawberries." I noticed from your Amazon profile that you frequently review gardening books. If you think you might be interested in reading my book and posting an honest review of it on Amazon, I'll gladly send a complimentary copy if you'll reply with your postal mailing address. There is no obligation, of course.

Best Regards

Carefully screen out reviewers whose profile indicates they aren't interested in your book's topic. In other words, don't send your fiction title to a reviewer whose profile says, "I review only nonfiction."

Only a small portion of Top Reviewers are likely to respond to your offer. Don't take a lack of response personally. Some reviewers are inundated with review copies from publishers who already have their mailing address and know their reading preferences, and simply don't have the time to reply.

Etiquette in Approaching Reviewers

Naturally, every author wants good reviews. And although it's perfectly ethical to seek reviews, don't do anything to suggest you're expecting favorable treatment. If you succeed in getting lots of reviews, you can expect that some of them will be negative.

"I see a fair number of books that I don't like, and I say so—including those sent to me as review copies," says Jane Corn, one of Amazon's Top 150 reviewers. "Anything else seems unethical to me."

Some Amazon Top Reviewers make it a practice not to review a book from a new author unless they can honestly recommend it to others and give it a rating of at least three or four stars out of five. Fortunately, many Top Reviewers make it a habit to avoid posting a review in cases where they simply hate the book. Sometimes reviewers are willing to give prepublication feedback, providing valuable advice on fixing a book's weaknesses. Sometimes such criticism can sting, and it can be hard to accept it gracefully. Try hard.

Yes, criticism sometimes hurts, but it lends credibility to your book, Corn says:

"Readers are smart. They can figure out who to trust, and those are the reviewers you want to reach. Always be clear about your willingness to have a fair, honest review. Anything else is self-defeating."

Finding More Amazon Reviewers

Another valuable source of potential reviewers is people who've posted Amazon reviews for books by others in your topic or genre. You can contact them using the same techniques mentioned above. Many reviewers list their "real" names and hometown on their Amazon profile, and with those two pieces of information, you can often locate them on Facebook. (You are on Facebook, aren't you? As you'll see several more times in this book, a Facebook account is a powerful tool for authors promoting their books online.)

Yes, finding volunteers to read and review your book is a long, tedious process but it can be well worth the effort. If you spend two or three days inviting about 100 to 200 potential Amazon reviewers to review your book, you can expect to receive about 25 or 30 responses, and wind up with perhaps a couple dozen reviews. If you get that many, consider your efforts a success.

Don't be tempted to ask for reviews from people who haven't actually read your book, even your mother. The result will be an unconvincing review that will detract from your book's credibility rather than bolster it.

Amazon Vine: Amazon invites customers who've posted numerous helpful reviews to join its "Vine" program, which provides access to free samples of new books and other products, sometimes before they're offered for sale. A Vine review is identical to reviews by other customers except that it's accompanied by a green "Vine Voice" badge.

Currently Amazon Vine is unavailable to small publishers. Vine is offered only to large vendors who pay hefty fees—several thousand dollars per title—in co-op advertising fees to Amazon. So if your book is self-published or submitted through a small press, you'll need to find reviewers by your own initiative.

Amazon invites customers to become Vine Voices based on their reviewer rank, which is a reflection of the quality and helpfulness of their reviews as judged by other Amazon customers. Amazon does not modify or edit Vine reviews, as long as they comply with the posting guidelines that apply to all customer reviews:

www.amazon.com/review-guidelines

Vine members receive a monthly newsletter via e-mail listing several books and other products that have been provided by the vendors. It's first come, first served—and the supply of popular items can be exhausted within minutes.

More Ways to Get Reviews

Once your book is selling, you'll have a steady stream of potential reviewers. Whenever you receive favorable comments or e-mails from readers, it's a chance to solicit a review. For example, if you receive an e-mail with a favorable comment about your book, you might include this in your response:

Thank you for the kind words about my book. It would be a tremendous help if you could post a summary of your thoughts as a Customer Review at Amazon.com to let readers know why you liked it.

Here's a link to post your review:

http://www.Amazon.com/gp/customer-reviews/write-a-review.html?asin=XXX

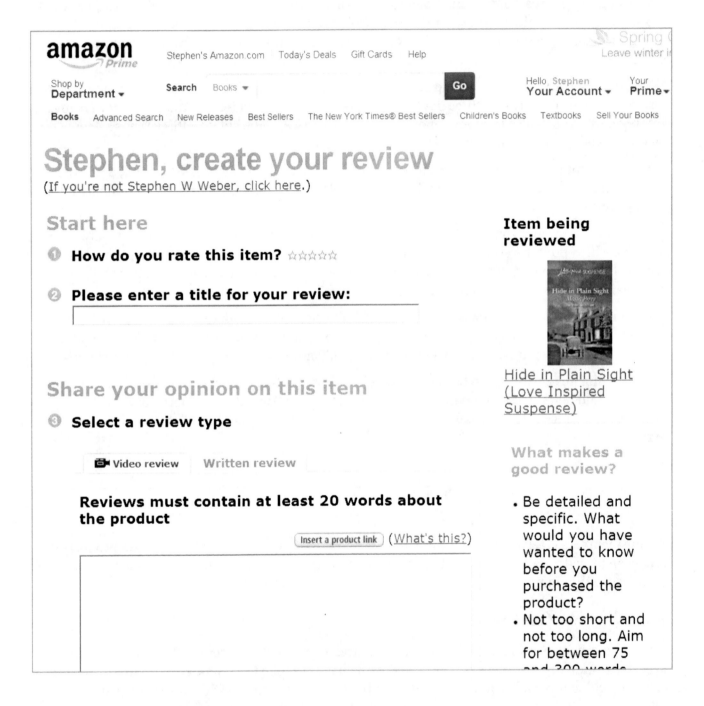

The link at the bottom takes the reader directly to Amazon's review form for your book. To customize the link for your book, replace the last three characters, XXX, in the link shown above with your book's 10-digit ISBN number. If you're unsure of your ISBN, consult the Amazon page for your book. Scroll about halfway down the page to the "Product Details" section and you'll see the ISBN, sometimes called the "ASIN." Use the 10-digit number (not the 13-digit version) and use numerals only (no dashes).

Amazon "Most Helpful" Reviews

Popular books on Amazon can draw dozens or even hundreds of reviews. But no matter how many reviews a book gets, three reviews have a special impact. Those three reviews are rated "Most Helpful" as a result of voting by Amazon shoppers answering "Yes" or "No" to the question appearing beneath each review, "Was this review helpful to you?" Reviews voted helpful most often are displayed in their entirety on the book's main Amazon page. Other reviews are excerpted in the right column.

Because they're usually the first bit of independent information buyers see about your book, those three "most helpful" reviews are crucial. Many browsers skim just those three reviews before deciding whether to buy.

"Most Helpful" reviews aren't designated until your book has several reviews that have received votes. Early on, new reviews appear on top, bumping earlier reviews down a notch. Subsequent reviews appear in reverse chronological order after the trio of "Most Helpful" reviews. Reviewers can't vote on their own reviews.

Negative Reviews

Positive reviews certainly help your book, but negative reviews on Amazon can have a bigger impact, according to a study by the Yale School of Management. Multiple glowing reviews for a book tend to be dismissed by shoppers as "hype" generated by the author or publisher, the study found. Negative reviews, however, are taken more seriously because buyers usually believe they represent honest criticism from disappointed readers.

Buyers understand that no book pleases everyone, and that any book reviewed often enough will get an occasional thumbs-down. But in some cases, a single detailed, critical review can devastate sales on Amazon, particularly with nonfiction how-to books.

The study, "The Effect of Word of Mouth on Sales: Online Book Reviews," examined random titles from Global Books in Print and bestsellers from *Publishers Weekly*. You can read the entire study here:

www.WeberBooks.com/reviews.pdf

Although customer reviews are one of Amazon's most valuable features, it was an innovation that irritated publishers in Amazon's early days, recalls chief executive Jeff Bezos:

> "We had publishers writing to us, saying, 'Why in the world would you allow negative reviews? Maybe you don't understand your business—you make money when you *sell things*. Get rid of the negative reviews, and leave the positive ones.'"

But negative reviews (and whether they appear informed and credible) help people decide what to buy, Bezos concludes: "We don't make money when we sell things; we make money when we help people make purchase decisions."

Customer Reviews

★★★★★ (9)
4.8 out of 5 stars

5 star		7
4 star		2
3 star		0
2 star		0
1 star		0

See all 9 customer reviews

" *I always enjoy reading Diane Moody's books.* "
Carol D. Hardin | 5 reviewers made a similar statement

" *I look forward to reading more from her!* "
Sharon Samms | 1 reviewer made a similar statement

" *Good character development and believable plot.* "
lindy | 2 reviewers made a similar statement

Most Helpful Customer Reviews

4 of 4 people found the following review helpful

★★★★★ **Another fun installment in the Tea Cup Novellas!** March 16, 2013

By S Wilson

Format: Kindle Edition

What do you get when you mix a straying congressman, a pierced and Harley-lovin' ex-pastor, and a sister who waits for furniture to speak to her? You get another fun adventure by Diane Moody. This time Tracey Collins leaves behind a fast-paced lifestyle in DC and makes her way back to Walnut Ridge...with a little romance on the way. Collect all the Teacup Novellas and experience each individual story sweetened with love!

Comment | Was this review helpful to you? Yes No

3 of 3 people found the following review helpful

★★★★★ **excellent read!** March 26, 2013

By Sharon Samms

Format: Kindle Edition | Amazon Verified Purchase

This is the 3rd novella I've read in The Teacup Novellas series & I've loved every one of them! If you're looking for great books you can't put down from beginning to end, these 3 books are for you! I look forward to reading more from her!

Comment | Was this review helpful to you? Yes No

3 of 3 people found the following review helpful

★★★★★ **Once Again, Diane** March 17, 2013

By Debbie

Format: Kindle Edition

Once again Diane, you have written another fun and touching Tea Cup novella! As in each one, the characters become the reader's friends.

Midway down a book's Amazon page you'll see the "most helpful" reviews on the left, and links to other reviews on the right.

Countering Malicious Reviews

Amazon polices its book review system but depends on community members to report abuses. Because Amazon reviews can be posted anonymously, nothing prevents the occasional malicious review or practical joke. In one well-known case, a prankster ridiculed Microsoft, then signed the review "Bill Gates," the name of the company's founder.

Familiarize yourself with Amazon's guidelines for acceptable reviews so you can request that its Community Help department delete inappropriate reviews. Generally, Amazon requires reviews to critique the book itself. Reviews that focus on the author or outside topics are often deleted.

You can review the guidelines here:

www.amazon.com/review-guidelines

Amazon also deletes reviews deemed "illegal, obscene, threatening, defamatory, invasive of privacy, infringing of intellectual property rights, or otherwise injurious to third parties." It also prohibits "political campaigning, commercial solicitation, chain letters, mass mailings, or any form of 'spam.'"

Reviewers are prohibited from impersonating other persons or using profanity, obscenities, spiteful remarks, phone numbers, mail addresses, URLs, product pricing and availability, alternative ordering or shipping information, or solicitations for helpful "votes" for reviews. Amazon has also been known to delete negative reviews posted by competing authors, reviews that contain inaccurate information about the author or publisher, and off-topic reviews.

You can request deletion of an inappropriate review on Amazon by contacting Amazon's staff via e-mail using the form on this page:

www.amazon.com/contactus

To ensure your complaint reaches the correct department, indicate your message is a "non-order" question, and then you'll be able to select "Customer Reviews" from a drop-down menu. Specify the book title, ISBN, the pen name of the reviewer, the first sentence of the review, and the date it was posted. State why you believe the review is inappropriate, and you should receive a reply within a few days.

Sometimes, no matter how inappropriate a review might be and how strongly you object, Amazon declines to delete it—and you're stuck with it. In that case, I offer these words of solace: There is no such thing as a "bad" review. Just as the old show-business expression, there's no such thing as "bad" publicity. Any review brings more attention to your book, which will succeed or fail on its own merits, independent of any single unflattering review. A negative review is better than nothing; it shows that your book is important enough for generate opinions. And everyone, no matter how wrongheaded or rude they are, has an opinion.

Old-Media Book Reviews

Most newspapers and magazines have reduced the space they allocate for book reviews in recent years, even as the number of books published has skyrocketed. Many of the remaining review columns are syndicated by national writers, leaving little opportunity for new authors to get reviewed, even in local media.

So if you're not famous already, the chances of your book being reviewed in a major traditional media outlet are worse than your chances of winning the lottery. But that's no reason to abandon the idea.

If more than three months remain before your book's publication date, you can submit it for consideration in these major trade review publications:

American Library Association's Booklist Online:

www.booklistonline.com/get-reviewed

800-545-2433

Kirkus Reviews:

www.Kirkusreviews.com/kirkusreviews/about_us/submission.jsp

212-777-4554

Library Journal:

reviews.libraryjournal.com/about/submitting-titles-for-review

212-463-6823

Publishers Weekly:

www.publishersweekly.com/pw/corp/submissionguidelines.html

212-645-9700

Midwest Book Review:

www.midwestbookreview.com/get_rev.htm

608-835-7937

Self-published authors get special consideration from Midwest Book Review, which also gives special preference to small presses and members of the Publishers Marketing Association. If your book is selected, its review will be posted to online retailers, relevant Web sites and forums, and included on an interactive CD-ROM provided to corporate, academic and public library systems.

More Review Opportunities

Perhaps a more realistic strategy for obtaining reviews in print media is to target specialized magazines and trade publications in your niche. You can find such publications by consulting the *Gale Directory of Publications and Broadcast Media*, available in many larger libraries. Another valuable resource is the Gebbie Press *All-In-One Media Directory*, which lists 24,000 outlets, including newspapers, magazines and radio stations. You can purchase and download lists of contacts at www.GebbieInc.com.

Sometimes, feature sections of newspapers—such as the Lifestyle, Home or Business sections—are more likely to feature a book, especially one by a local author.

Posting Trade Reviews on Amazon

As mentioned in the previous chapter, Amazon's Author Central licenses prepublication reviews from major trade publications, so if you have secured these reviews, ensure they appear on your title's Amazon detail page. For reviews published in newspapers or other publications for which Amazon doesn't license reprints, you can condense the review to 20 words and Amazon will republish the summary on your book's detail page, relying on the "fair use" exemption of copyright law.

Amazon will display a maximum of 10 published reviews on your book's detail page.

Fee-Based Book Reviews

Considering the work involved in getting book reviews, more authors than ever are willing to pay for them. Several fee-based review services have popped up in recent years, primarily to serve self-publishing authors who are effectively locked out of traditional book reviews.

Many publishing veterans believe that paid reviews are ineffective and unethical, and I tend to agree with them. But that hasn't stopped several companies from offering paid reviews, even respected companies such as Kirkus and Bowker.

Kirkus offers "Indie" reviews for around $400. A "ForeWord" Clarion Review costs about the same. But, believe me, people know the difference between a real book review and one that's been paid for. Most authors who've bought a paid review will tell you it didn't do a darned thing for their sales. And Amazon's staff has been known to delete paid reviews posted by fly-by-night operators.

Critics argue these paid reviews aren't read by consumers, and that their supposed target audience—booksellers and librarians—pay no attention to paid reviews.

"I feel that paying for book reviews is a bad idea," says self-publishing guru Dan Poynter. "There's a compromise there. And people can see right through it—they know it's a paid review, so it's an ad."

Jim Cox, editor in chief of Midwest Book Review, puts it even more bluntly:

"Any reviewer that wants money from you for any purpose whatsoever is operating a scam—engaging in unethical behavior that is in violation of the publishing industry etiquette and norm."

Traditional Media Interviews

Landing national media exposure can greatly enhance your book sales, but many new authors don't have the resources to hire a publicist. One way to get exposure in newspapers, radio and television without hiring a publicist is www.PRLeads.com. Several times a day, users receive a list of queries from journalists looking for expert sources for the stories they're writing.

On a typical day, a PRLeads subscriber might see a query like this:

SUBJECT:

BUSINESS: Small Companies Going into International Markets – Boston Daily News

For a national newspaper, I'm writing a story on how small-business owners should make the decision to go into international markets. What factors should they consider? How can they evaluate the opportunity? How soon after establishing yourself domestically should you consider this? I'm looking for comments from experts, and examples of entrepreneurs who have been dealing with this issue.

Authors and experts with relevant expertise could send this reporter a brief e-mail, describing their credentials and how they can address the topic. Later, the reporter might follow up via phone or e-mail for an interview. Subscriptions to PRLeads cost $99 a month. For more information, see:

www.PRLeads.com/pr-leads-faq.htm

Here's a similar service that charges no fees: "Help a Reporter Out" or HARO for short. The HARO website claims they offer more than 100,000 sources around the world looking to be quoted in the media. They send out over 1,200 queries from worldwide media each week. Promising that they will not otherwise use or sell your information, authors may register with HARO online with a form. Once registered, HARO will send you e-mails listing stories reporters are working on and what kinds of expert advice they need. Does the story fit in with your area of expertise? Even better, is it on topic with your book?

HARO provides a web form that you can use to contact the reporter you might be able to help and pitch yourself as a quotable expert to them. If these reporters quote you in their story, it's free publicity. If the story mentions your book title, even better. In any case, you're burnishing your reputation as an expert in your field. This will prompt more writers and reporters to seek you out, enhancing your expert status. For more information about HARO, see:

www.helpareporter.com/

Press Releases

A press release is a pseudo-news story written in the third person, seeking to demonstrate to an editor or reporter the newsworthiness of a particular person, event, service or product.

Not too long ago, press releases were terribly expensive because they had to be mailed—or faxed or wire-delivered—to traditional media outlets like newspapers. Then your message would reach a gatekeeper, like an editor, who might decide to trash your release. If your release were used at all, the finished article could be totally different from your intended message and your name or book title might not even appear.

Now, dozens of inexpensive and free press-release distribution services can make your announcement visible to the entire world, exactly as you wrote it. For an additional fee of about $40, these services will post your news to sites like Google News, Yahoo News and others, providing even wider exposure.

When writing a press release, the most important thing is to focus on the *reader*, not on you or your book. For example, what problem does your book solve for the reader, or what kind of entertainment does it provide? Nobody wants to read an announcement that simply says Mrs. Y wrote a book about Topic X. Who cares? Tell your audience *what's in it for them.*

Here's an effective (but fictionalized) book press release that generates interest by focusing on readers:

"American parents are furious with Hollywood for glamorizing stick-thin bodies, and many girls say they're self-conscious about their bodies as a result of movies, television and magazines. This national obsession with thinness is resulting in eating disorders and depression among millions of teens, according to Anita Jones, author of *Nourishing Girls: Help Your Teen Develop Self-Esteem and a Healthy Body Image....*"

And here's the other side of the coin, a release that induces boredom by focusing solely on the author and what he's pushing:

"In a newly released political thriller, ex-diplomat, military intelligence officer, college football standout and news reporter James McNeil authentically captures the hardball maneuverings and virtual mortality of Washington power politics. Critics give two thumbs up to *Shotgun Diplomacy*, the author's second novel...."

Yawn...

Here are some recommended press release distribution services:

www.prweb.com (formerly www.eMediaWire.com) is a popular channel of press release distribution for many authors and publishers announcing new titles.

www.PRNewswire.com

www.BusinessWire.comwww.Send2Press.com

www.PRLeap.com

www.eReleases.com

Well known British PR firm Vitis recently studied the use of press release services in the UK—both paid and free. They also surveyed journalists to find out which newswires they actually read. The results of the studies in a nutshell:

Paid press release services are effective but very expensive. Their teams will generally correct and approve your release, making sure it is well written and free from libel, and distribute it to newswires within 15 minutes of contracting them. They offer translation services for international releases and some of them offer a report, for an extra charge, showing where your story was picked up.

Free press release services can be helpful for getting your story mentioned by Google News and for appearing in web searches, but not in reaching journalists, bloggers, editors and other influencers. The latter simply don't have time to browse unfiltered press releases. If they use them at all, it's for monitoring industry trends at their leisure—not under deadline.

To read the report in full, visit http://www.vitispr.com/blog/effective-press-releases.

Building Your Author Platform

If you are selling your book on Amazon—and everyone should—you already have a web presence there: your Author Profile page which you have built with Author Central. If you are taking advantage of social media, especially Facebook—and everyone should—you already have your Author and/or Book pages there. So, do you need a website, too?

No, you don't necessarily need a separate website. But having one has many advantages. It creates a central location for your entire writing business that is all about you, and is solely under your control, and is not subject to the whims of Amazon or Facebook. Your Web presence provides a landing place for anyone who wants to get to know you better as they explore your writing. And it is a way to organize information about all your books and all the ways people can buy and read them, in one place.

Many authors use a "blog" as their website, and we'll explore blogs in detail in the following chapter.

Building Blocks of Your Presence

The great thing about a Web site is you can always add to it. Here are some basic elements you'll want to consider adding to your site:

- Content: nobody will visit a site that's merely an advertisement for your book. Your content can be a series of articles, book excerpts, or even feedback from your readers. If your website includes a blog, consider the blog your main content.

- Book cover artwork, description, and excerpts

- Your biography

- Links to purchase your book, either on your site or online retailers such as Amazon and Barnes & Noble. The more choices you offer buyers, the better. In most states you can earn referral money for directing a buyer to Amazon or Barnes & Noble from your website if the referral results in a purchase.

- Reviews of your book

- A form where visitors can enter their e-mail address to subscribe to a newsletter or site updates. (Speaking of e-mail newsletters, two mailing services I can recommend are Mailchimp.com and Aweber.com)

- Contact information: your e-mail address (or a form that forwards messages) and perhaps postal address and phone number

- A "media room" with any press releases announcing your book or any news coverage involving you or your book

- Suggested interview questions, along with your responses

Before you begin planning your site, consider your target audience and what type of information you want to give them. Will your site be a topic-driven site, or a personality-driven site? Topic-driven sites usually work best for nonfiction, and if you continue writing related books, you'll have a built-in audience for those new books. Personality-driven sites can work well for fiction writers and those with famous names.

Whatever your approach, the goal is to provide content your target audience finds worthwhile.

Waiting for Results

Building a Web site can be a lonely process, much like the early phases of writing a manuscript. Don't expect a big response in the first month or even the next six months. Often it takes an entire year for an author site or blog to gain momentum. But if you concentrate on producing a useful site with quality content, word will get around.

As you build your site, keep one general idea in mind: Unless you're already a superstar, don't make your Web site about *you*. Make it about *the reader*. Provide compelling content that is related to what you write about—content that solves problems, entertains, sparks curiosity, or inspires. Everything else will follow.

Resist the temptation to pack your site with fancy features like flashy graphics or voices or music that plays automatically. Usually, these doodads have the opposite effect than what was intended—they make your site slow, irritating, noisy and hard to read.

When to Launch Your Site

Launch your site as soon as you can. It's impossible to be too early, and it's never too late. By all means, don't wait until your book's publication date. Having a Web site is not only a valuable tool for publicizing a book, but for writing a book, too, because it keeps you in touch with readers. More on that later.

"The best time to start promoting your book is three years before it comes out," says bestselling author Seth Godin. "Three years to build a reputation, build a permission asset, build a blog, build a following, build credibility, and build the connections you'll need later."

A permission asset is something like a list of friends and contacts that have given you permission to contact them. These will hopefully be your most loyal customers.

Blogging for Authors

Julie Powell moved to New York to become an actress. A few years later, she realized she was 30 years old, working a dead-end job to pay the bills, and still had no acting prospects. Then, on a visit to Texas, she borrowed her mother's copy of Julia Child's landmark 1961 cookbook, *Mastering the Art of French Cooking, Volume 1*. Back in her cramped kitchen on Long Island, Powell cooked one of the recipes for her husband, who enjoyed it so much he urged her to attend culinary school and become a professional cook.

Instead, Powell decided to teach herself, and let the whole world watch. She vowed to cook each of the book's 524 recipes during the following year, and write a diary about it on a Web log, or *blog*. Powell wrote about killing lobsters, boiling calves' hooves, and making homemade mayonnaise, but she didn't confine herself to cooking. For good measure, she heaped on details of her sex life, recipes for reviving a romance, and snide remarks about her backstabbing coworkers.

Powell began one entry: "My husband almost divorced me last night, and it was all because of the sauce tartar." Her storytelling was so good, word got around fast and thousands began reading her blog—regardless of whether they cared about French cuisine. A write-up in the *New York Times* brought thousands more readers.

By the time Powell was winding down her project, publishers were knocking on the door with book contracts, and her blog turned into the bestselling book, *Julie and Julia: 365 Days, 524 Recipes, 1 Tiny Apartment Kitchen* and, more recently, a major motion picture starring Meryl Streep. More than 100,000 copies of the book sold its first year, a monster success for any memoir, let alone a book by an unknown, chronically unemployed actress.

Blogging is a relatively easy way for you to publicize your book and even improve your writing while you're at it. If you can write an e-mail, you can write a blog—it's the easiest, cheapest, and perhaps best way for authors to find an audience and connect with readers. Blogging is an informal, intimate form of communication that inspires trust among your readers. You accomplish this by forming a sort of relationship with your readers, who learn that they can expect quality content and frequent postings.

For the same reasons that traditional advertising is usually ineffective for selling books, a blog can be highly effective for book promotion. People interested in your topic seek out your message.

What Is a Blog?

Put simply, a blog is a Web site with a few interactive features. You don't have to call it a blog unless you want to. It's possible that within a few years, nearly every Web site will have interactive features, and people simply won't call them blogs anymore.

You needn't know anything about computers to blog. Simply type into a form, and presto—the whole world can see it. Your blog is a content management system—a painless way to build and maintain a platform where readers can discover and enjoy your writing.

A blog can be a part of your Web site, or it can be *the* Web site. The main thing that distinguishes a blog from a plain old Web site is that a blog is frequently updated with short messages, or *posts*. Readers often chime in with their own comments at the bottom of each post. This free exchange of ideas is what makes blogs a revolutionary tool for authors: A successful blog is a constant stream of ideas, inspiration, perspective, and advice—it's a real-time, global focus group.

Why Blogs Are Better

Some authors who already have a book for sale resist the idea of blogging and the "extra work" it entails. Their reasoning is, "Why create more deadlines when your book is already finished?"

Don't even go there. The thing about Author Blogs is that you are already a writer. Since you've made it your profession, the odds are that you are good at it or it comes easily to you—or both. Any business can benefit from having a blog to promote it, but not every business person is a writer. You are. And that is more than half the battle in creating and maintaining a blog.

If you're like most authors, the entire time you're writing your book you're thinking about your target audience, the reader. If you're writing non-fiction you might be hoping they heard you correctly and understood all you've wanted to convey. You might hope they have read your information and are on to the next steps—what they will do with it, after they read your book. If you're writing fiction you might be eager for feedback about your story—how they (hopefully) loved the book, who they recommended it to, what difference it ultimately made in their lives, and so on. Writing a blog, which opens a direct line of communication to readers and potential readers, can help you continue a conversation with your readers, and get new ones.

Besides all that, blogging can help you maximize the effectiveness of things you're probably already doing, like answering e-mails from your readers.

Compared with other types of Internet publicity content such as static Web sites or e-mail newsletters, blogs provide three big advantages:

- Blogs are easy to start and maintain.

- The short, serialized content of blogs encourages regular readership, repeated exposure to your books, and more sales.

- Blogs rank high in search-engine results from Google and other providers, making them easy to find.

Why do blogs get so much traffic from search engines? First, blogs are topical. When you're writing about the same topics and ideas day in and day out, your site becomes packed with the keywords your audience is searching for. Stay at it awhile, and it becomes nearly impossible for your target audience to miss you, thanks to Google and the other search engines. Most new visitors will find your site by using a search engine, after looking for words and topics contained in your Web pages.

Another reason blogs are so easy to find is that search engines usually rank them higher than other types of Web sites. Thus your links can show up at the top of search results, which is where most people click.

Google and the other search engines give extra credit to blogs for a couple of reasons:

- Blogs are updated frequently, and the assumption is "fresh" content is more valuable.

- Blogs tend to have many links from other Web pages with similar content. The assumption is that because other bloggers and Webmasters have decided to link to your content, it's probably valuable.

Your visibility in search results is key, since about 40 percent of your new visitors will likely arrive via a Web search. If your site ranks highly in Web searches for the keywords related to your book, you'll have a constant source of well-qualified visitors and likely book buyers.

Breathing the Blogosphere

Step 1 in becoming a blogger is to consume some blogs yourself. Reading other blogs gives you a quick feel for what works, what doesn't, and the techniques you'll want to apply to your own blog.

A handy tool for keeping track of all the blogs you like and will want to visit frequently is a *newsreader* or *aggregator*, which saves you the trouble of poking around the Web, looking for new blog posts. Instead, your newsreader gathers and displays updates for you. One free, easy-to-use reader is Feedly.com. For more information, see:

www.feedly.com

Sign up for a Feedly account and then whenever you find a blog you'd like to subscribe to and read often, just a few clicks subscribes you to that blog. From that point on, all new posts for it and all the other blogs or websites you like to read, are collected and kept on one page that you can visit and read at your leisure.

Another free reader is Bloglines; it works in much the same way.

www.Bloglines.com

Besides reading and following blogs you like, you will want to interact with them. Your own, as well as most of the blogs you will likely want to connect with, will be hosted either by Blogger or WordPress. They each ask you to register an account with them, and you should. Of course, you will already have an account with the one you are using for your own blog, but go ahead and register for the other one, too. When you register, you will get a username and part of your user profile will be a link back to your own blog. So, when other bloggers read your thoughtful and interesting comments, they can click on your profile to find out who you are and will then be directed to your own blog.

There are millions of blogs, and finding ones that suit you can be like searching for a needle in a haystack. There's no easy way to filter out low-quality blogs—you've just got to sample what's out there.

Building your list of target blogs requires some legwork because there is no current, comprehensive directory of all blogs. To determine the popularity, authority and quality of blogs in your niche, you'll need to sample the content yourself.

Start your search here:

www.Technorati.com This blog tracking site lists the top 100 most popular blogs at Technorati.com/pop/blogs. But to find niche content, you'll need to look beyond these mainstream blogs. Consult the advanced search tool, Technorati.com/search, where you can drill down into specific topics.

www.google.com/blogsearch Type in keywords related to your book. Ignore results from personal blogs that focus on the author and get little traffic.

There is a wealth of information online on the subject of blogs, and since online journalists love to make lists, you can do a web search such as "best author blogs" and start looking there.

Another good place to find high quality blogs is by visiting the site that keeps track of the best: The Weblog Awards, also known as The Bloggies. You will find hundreds of sections for blogs that have been voted by the online community in categories such as Best Writing, Best Designed, Best New Blog, etc. You can find The Bloggies here:

http://2013.bloggi.es

Once you've identified some blogs in your area of interest, jump on the band wagon. Find the most popular, most-visited blogs among them. Start following those blogs and leave thoughtful comments on their posts. This is a good thing to do, because Bloggers know that the more followers they have, the better. So once you begin following their blog, many will reciprocate by following yours. If they don't, feel free to leave a comment next time telling them how you found their blog—whether through a link from another blogger or a comment they left on another blog you both read, or their book page of Amazon—and add these words: *I'm you're newest follower; I hope you'll visit my blog and follow me back.* Here are some examples of popular author blogs:

Jennifer Weiner

Bestselling author Jennifer Weiner, whose novel *In Her Shoes* was recently made into a major motion picture starring Cameron Diaz, Toni Collette and Shirley McLaine, maintains a free blog on Blogger which can be found on her website. See http://jenniferweiner.blogspot.com/

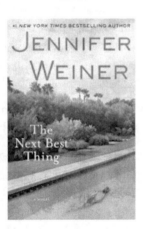

THE NEXT BEST THING — In Stores July 3rd!

Wednesday, October 03, 2012
posted by Jen at 10/03/2012 10:39:00 PM

My goodness! October already!

It's been a busy few months around here, right?

My kids started school. Then they both got lice. I feel like my life has been an endless cycle of combing, rinsing, washing, and calling the professional nit-pickers.

I went on "The Today Show," where I talked about un-kosher chickens and sanitary napkins and why women are so hard on each other about baby weight, and how that really needs to stop. Missed it? Here's the link!

Welcome to *A Moment of Jen*, author Jennifer Weiner's constantly-updated take on books, baby, and news of the world. Email me at jen (a) jenniferweiner.com.

JenniferWeiner.com
Facebook
Follow me on Twitter

To order Then Came You, click on the cover

To order Fly Away Home, click on the cover

To order Best Friends Forever, click on the cover

Weiner blogs about being a writer and a mother, and how that is working out for her. She uses her blog to promote her books, have contests and giveaways, and vent about the inequality she believes exists in the world of writing awards. When you read her blog, you feel as if she is your friend. Because she writes what is referred to as Chick Lit and her audience is women like her, that is very effective.

Dr. Frank's Whats-It.

Musician and author Frank Portman, whose band MTX has been making albums and touring since the 1980s, blogs at doktorfrank.com. He creates a way for fans of his book and his music to connect with him by inviting them to e-mail him a photo of them reading one of his novels, which he then posts on his blog.

http://www.doktorfrank.com/

Jessica Crispin

You can't get much more authorcentric than Bookslut.com. Blogger Jessica Crispin recreated herself as an expert on all things bookish when she started blogging about books in 2002. She now runs Bookslut, arguably the most popular eZine and website about books in the world.

Marion Nestle, the author of Food Politics, blogs regularly on the topic. In doing so, this noted expert in the field keeps you current on what she's reading/listening to/watching on the subject. See www.foodpolitics.com.

Once you've found a few blogs of interest, it's easy to find more. Bloggers tend to link to one another, both within their blog posts, and often within a side menu of links known as a *blogroll*. And, because bloggers read blogs, try that trick of clicking on the profiles of the commenters to see their blog.

You will also find many opportunities to participate in "blog parties" or other online events where a day is set aside for many blogs to post about the same subject and then link up to each other. You might even find a weekly "party" that fits your book's subject and has a following, which is a great opportunity to publicize your blog. For example, did you write a cookbook? There are many link parties associated with food, entertaining, tablesetting design, kid-friendly meals, etc. If you are a foodie, you could probably publish blog posts just about daily by only participating in blog parties—but don't. Your blog needs to have varied and interesting content in between to keep readers coming back.

Getting Started

You could pay a lot of money to an Internet consultant to custom-build a website or blog, but many free alternatives are available:

Blogger.com Owned by Google, Blogger is perhaps the most widely known and feature-rich free blogging platform. You can choose from a few different templates and customize your blog according to your taste in fonts, background images, and colors. You simply type into the Web form, push the "publish" button, and your blog post appears.

WordPress.com This free blogging platform has a steeper learning curve than Blogger, but offers more flexibility and control over the appearance of your blog. Although it's free to use the WordPress platform, you might decide to pay for some upgraded features. You can use Wordpress.com for a basic blog, or a full-fledged website. If you choose Wordpress, you'll be in good company. Some famous names, like Time, CNN, and TechCrunch use Wordpress for their sites.

There is another type of Wordpress blog available that offers more flexibility but is more complicated to start. It's known as a "self-hosted" Wordpress installation. These types of plans start at just a few dollars per month. You can get more information from popular Web hosting companies such as Bluehost and Go Daddy, and more information about self-hosting Wordpress here:

http://www.godaddy.com/hosting/wordpress-hosting.aspx

http://www.bluehost.com/wordpress

Tumblr.com

Here's a nice service that fits especially well with bloggers who post short messages along with artwork or photography, sometimes called "micro-blogging." Tumblr is popular because it so easily integrates with social networking sites like Facebook, which is important if your target audience is the younger set. If the concept is new to you, check out Tumblr's "About Page," which explains it nicely:

www.tumblr.com/about

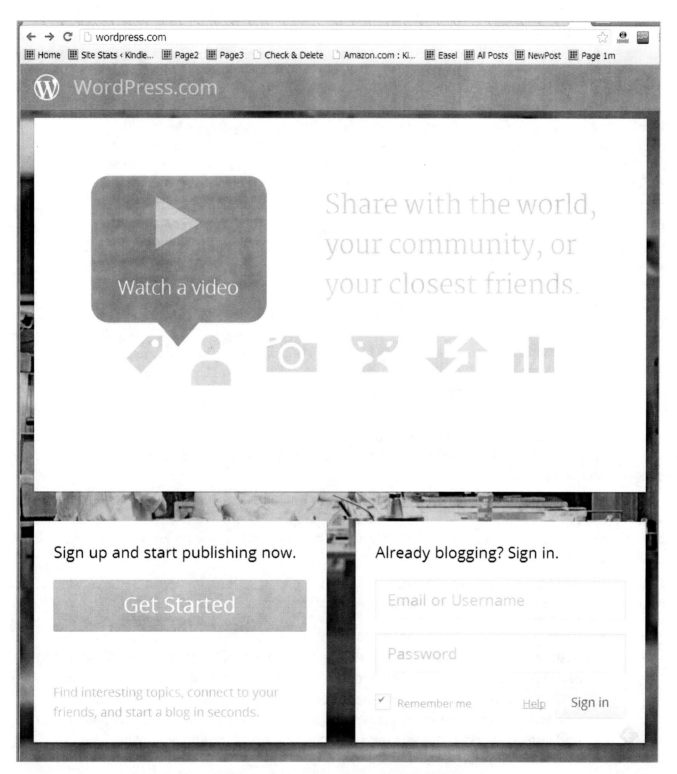

You can start a blog within five minutes at Wordpress.com.

Since Tumblr has become popular, some bloggers have a Tumblr blog as well as a regular blog—simply to drive traffic to their regular blog. You can post one photo and a short note to Tumblr and then direct readers to your off-Tumblr blog.

Your Blog's Title

A blog title usually spans the top portion of each page like a newspaper masthead. Titles are usually short and catchy—perhaps just a couple of nonsense words like *Boing Boing*, or a made-up compound word like *RocketBoom* or *BuzzMachine*. The name could be a non sequitur or double-entendre like *PostSecret*. Sometimes a title is just a title, like *The Official Google Weblog*.

Try to include in your title the most critical keyword related to your niche. *Joe's Organic Strawberry Growing, Baking and Eating Guide* is a good title. A poor title would be *Joe's Thoughts and Ideas about Fruit* because nobody would search for something like that, and if they saw it, they couldn't guess what it's about. Be obvious. Pick a few words that will be easy for people to remember and to repeat in conversation and e-mails.

Connecting with Readers

It's natural to be apprehensive about starting a blog. When you first begin, it may feel like being on stage without a script or a view of the audience. Don't worry, feedback will come soon enough. Remember, there's no right or wrong way to blog. The only rule is your target audience must find something worthwhile.

Good blogs are addictive, which is one reason they're so effective for authors. Many book buyers must be exposed to a title six or seven times before deciding to buy. With a good blog, getting repeated exposure won't be a problem.

A lively blog is like a focus group and writing laboratory rolled into one; it provides you with constant feedback, criticism and new ideas. Your blog readers will pepper you with comments and e-mails. When you've struck a chord, you'll know immediately from the response. When you lay an egg, you'll know that, too, from the silence.

Just as theater companies try out new productions in the hinterlands before storming Broadway, authors can fine-tune their material on their blog, says technology writer Clive Thompson:

> "Ask writers who blog regularly—like me—and they'll tell you how exciting it is to be wired in directly to your audience. They correspond with you, pass you tips, correct your factual blunders, and introduce you to brilliant new ideas and people. The Internet isn't just an audience, it's an auxiliary brain. But you have to turn it on, and it takes work. You can't fake participation and authenticity online."

Indeed, the true power of blogging is the momentum created by your audience. Once your blog has 100 frequent readers, it has critical mass. It may take six months or a year to get there, but from there it's all downhill. Members of your core audience begin competing to hand you the most useful, compelling ideas by writing comments on your blog and e-mailing you directly. That's when your blog comes alive, like a magnet attracting new readers. Your core audience swells as word of mouth goes viral.

Blog Style

Just as every book and author is unique, there's an endless variety of blog styles and flavors. All the blogging services have page templates, allowing you to start with a basic design and add a few personal elements.

Don't get bogged down looking for the "perfect" design. You'll always be free to tweak your design or do a complete overhaul later. The most important thing is to get started adding content and building your audience.

The main design requirement is readability. Plain vanilla blogs are fine, and are actually preferred by most readers—it's the words that count. Black text on a white background might seem uninspired, but it's much easier on the eyes than white text on a black background or some other color. A plain masthead with your blog title in simple capital letters is fine to start. The important thing is to get started.

A nonfiction author's blog can approach the topic from several directions:

- New developments

- New products or services

- Hot-button issues of the day

- What other blogs or media are saying

- Reviews of new books in the field

You can publish a blog in the style of a perpetual newsletter or an aggregation of interesting tidbits about your book's topic. As you notice new things and write about them, each post is stacked on top, and with each new post added on top, one of the older posts is bumped from the bottom and sent to your archives.

Let's imagine you're writing a blog on the topic of organic strawberries. Your blog could serve as an information clearinghouse covering every conceivable angle and trend of organic strawberry growing, cooking and consuming. You'll constantly monitor consumer and trade media for the latest news on organic growing, interpret this material for your audience, and link to the source material, adding your own commentary.

Your blog could include:

- Questions from your blog readers on organic fruit, along with your answers

- Guest articles from experts on organic strawberry gardening

- New books and magazines on the topic

- Strawberry dessert recipes

- The best places to grow organic strawberries

- Listings and maps of markets offering organic strawberries

- Reviews of cookbooks addressing natural, organic, fruit and dessert preparation

Fiction authors have even more freedom, but they also have a bigger creative burden. They can write about themselves, or even from the point of view of a fictional character. A story from their book can continue on the blog, veering off in new directions, experimentally, in response to suggestions from readers and other writers. Often, avid readers are wannabe writers themselves, so writing about the creative process is something that can keep people interested and coming back for more.

Blog Comments: Pros and Cons

Most blogs include space below the author's posts for readers to add their own views. These comments can take the conversation in a totally new direction, and become the most interesting material on your blog, thanks purely to your readers' efforts.

For the blogger, comments bring three key benefits:

1. Instant feedback on your ideas and writing, and a sense of what your audience finds valuable

2. Feeling of participation and loyalty among your audience

3. Adding valuable keyword density to your site, making it much more visible in search-engine results

Commenting can be a two-way street. One way to build a following to your blog is to reply to comments as often as possible. You can set up your blog so that all comments are e-mailed to you, and then in most cases you need only hit "reply" to e-mail the person back. Readers love knowing that their comment was received and appreciated.

While this sounds like it could be a daunting task, bear in mind that in the beginning you probably won't be getting more than 10 comments on any given blog post, and hitting "reply" and sending a one or two sentence response to a thoughtful comment is well worth the investment in time if it brings you a loyal reader.

Like any tool, however, comments can be abused. It's not unusual to see rude or off-topic comments on some blogs, and even "spam comments" written solely to plant links back to the spammer's site. The worst spammers even use software robots, which scour the Web for target blogs and insert their junk links. Spam comments are usually along the lines of, "Hey, great blog. Come see us at www.Cheap-Viagra.com."

Fortunately, most problem comments can be prevented by using countermeasures like *comment moderation*. Here, you review and approve new comments before they appear on your blog. Another option is to allow readers to post comments immediately, and you review them later. The advantage is your readers get immediate gratification in seeing their comments posted as they submit them.

Most spam comments can be prevented by using *word verification*, requiring comment writers to type a short series of characters displayed in an image. This stops spam comments from software robots.

Blogger.com uses a sophisticated system, not unlike Google's gmail does, to predict which comments are spam and remove them to a Spam folder for you.

Writing Your Blog Posts

The essential ingredient of a blog is its short entries, or posts. They're arranged in reverse chronological order, with the newest at top. Posts can be a few sentences long, or many paragraphs long, and often link to outside information like blogs, newspaper stories, or multimedia clips hosted elsewhere on the Web.

Nearly any tidbit of information relevant to your audience can be spun into a blog post of some type:

- Informational: a news-oriented blurb or a new development

- Question/Answer: easy to write and fun to read; reliable material, even if you have to make up the question

- Instructional: can be a longer post, a tutorial that explains how to do something related to your niche

- Link posts: find an interesting blog post elsewhere and link to it, adding your own spin

- Rant: let off some steam and let it rip—interesting blogs don't play it safe, they take sides

- Book review: review a book related to your field—it can be a new book or a classic that newcomers haven't heard of

- Product reviews: the word "review" is a popular search term—give your frank opinion, and encourage your readers to chime in with their own views

- Lists: readers love lists so write about the "Top 5 Ways" to do a task, or the "Top 10 Reasons" for such-and-such; if someone else publishes a list, you can summarize it or critique it on your own blog

- Interviews: chat with someone in your field; provide a text summary on your blog; add a transcript or even an audio file

- Case studies: report on how so-and-so does such-and-such; you don't have to call it a "case study," just tell the story

- Profiles: focus on a particular person or personality; the person profiled can be someone well known in your field or perhaps a newcomer nobody's heard of

Most blogs are conversational and informal, but that doesn't give authors a license to be sloppy. Readers expect clear writing from an author, and that requires attention to detail—not to mention beginning your sentences with capital letters and ending them with periods. Resist any temptation toward "texting" abbreviations such as the letter "u" as a short form of the word "you."

It's worth proofreading and spell-checking your posts before publishing. Keeping your paragraphs short will minimize your rewriting chores.

Raw Materials for Posts

A free, easy way to find new raw material for your blog is to create a "Google Alert," which will automatically scour thousands of media sources for any keywords you specify. You'll be alerted via e-mail when something containing your keyword or words appear in newspapers, magazines, Web sites, or other sources. Sign up at:

www.Google.com/alerts

Google Alerts are also a handy way to monitor mentions of your blog title, book titles, and even your name or the names of other authors. An alternative to Google Alerts is Talkwalker, which is a good service for monitoring social media for certain keywords. See http://www.talkwalker.com.

Here are more ideas for generating content for your blog and other online communities:

- **Post question-and-answer content**. On your blog or Web site, summarize the best questions you receive from readers via e-mail, phone calls, letters or personal conversations. Publish them in a question-and-answer format. This provides interesting, valuable and easy-to-read content. Q&A content is simple to produce, especially if you're already producing the raw material by answering e-mails. When you post this content publicly, your entire audience benefits, instead of just one person (although you should omit any information that will personally identify anyone). Further, Q&As expand your audience because the format boosts your visibility with search engines. Many people searching the Web actually type questions into Google, such as "How to stop thumb-sucking." You can rewrite the questions for clarity, or even write the question yourself to help illustrate a point. You can use this same type of content to build an FAQ, or Frequently Asked Questions, page on your site.

- **Offer book excerpts or sample chapters.** Make this available as a PDF download from your Web site. At a minimum, you should offer your book's table of contents, index and a short excerpt. One popular science-fiction author, Cory Doctorow, provides free downloads of the entire text of all his novels at his site, www.CrapHound.com. The resulting publicity far outweighs the cost of any lost book sales, Doctorow says: "I'm more interested in getting more of that wider audience into the tent than making sure that everyone who's in the tent bought a ticket to be there."

- **Participate in online discussions.** Answering queries about your topic on discussion boards and e-mail lists can lure more visitors to your site. Find relevant groups on Web boards and in groups sponsored by Yahoo, MSN, LiveJournal and America Online. Add a three- or four-line signature to the bottom of your posts, including your Web address and current book title. Be sure to provide helpful information; don't post purely promotional messages. Follow the rules of the group, which sometimes preclude commercial content.

- **Post comments on blogs related to your topic.** While some disable the feature, many blogs allow you to include a link back to your site in your comment. Invest the time in providing useful, thoughtful commentary, and you'll bring some new visitors to your site.

Over the Long Haul

Blogs evolve and priorities change. It's impossible to draw up a road map for the future, but here are some strategic ideas to help give your blog long-term direction:

Write an *anchor* post every month or two. An anchor post is a tutorial-style piece that teaches your readers how to do something, like *How to Pick Fruit at its Peak of Flavor* or *Top 10 Ways to Prevent Identity Theft*. It can be the length of a short magazine article, perhaps 750 to 1,500 words. This type of content is evergreen—it won't become obsolete, and you can continually refer to it in your subsequent posts. Every month or two, add another anchor post.

Write at least one new post a day in the beginning. Frequent posting keeps your audience interested and jogs your creativity. The more you post, the more you'll be picked up by the search engines, and the more new people will find your blog, become regular readers and buy your book. The first two sentences are the hardest of a post, and it's all smooth sailing after that.

- **Comment on other blogs in your niche.** This will attract fellow bloggers and their readers who follow the link in your comment back to your blog. Make a meaningful comment that advances the discussion; don't just say "I agree."

- **Link to other blogs from within your blog posts.** With certain blogging software, this is known as a *trackback*, and leaves a summary of your blog post on the original blog. Result: more bloggers and readers find you.

- **Ask for comments on your blog.** End your posts with a question, prompting your readers for feedback. When practical, end your posts with a question like, "What do you think?" or "What's your take on this?" Readers are often more interested in what *they* have to say than in what *you* have to say.

- **Don't write when you're angry.** If you're upset, cool off for a few hours—or a day—before posting something nasty that you might regret later. It's nearly impossible to delete stuff on the Web. You might erase something from your blog, but the text can be archived in dozens of other places.

- **Link to your old content.** After you've been blogging for a while, you'll have five or six previous blog posts that were most popular with readers—drawing lots of links, traffic and comments. For the benefit of new readers, link to these previous posts when you write about the same topics in the future. Add a small menu of these posts on the sidebar of your blog, with a heading such as Lively Conversations or Greatest Hits.

- **Add artwork.** Sprinkling your own or stock photos and illustrations in your blog posts is a simple way to add visual appeal. Images are eyeball magnets. Writing a post about how to fix a flat tire? Include a small stock photo of someone installing a tire. The site www.sxc.hu has thousands of royalty-free photos you can search by keyword. You needn't illustrate your posts literally, which can get boring. Let's imagine your post concerns some type of *manipulation*. It's the key idea and the main word in your post title. How could you illustrate it? Just search for "manipulation" at the photo site mentioned above, and you'll see dozens of images you could use as a smart illustration—like photos of puppets, marionettes or chess pawns. If your first keyword doesn't find results, try a synonym. Or if you're feeling ironic, try an antonym.

More Blogging Fine Points:

- Write in the first person. Never talk about yourself as a different being.

- Write keyword-rich headlines. Give people a reason to start reading.

- Hook your audience in the first sentence. Ask a question or pose a challenge.

- Don't get too preachy. Blog communication isn't top-down, it's a conversation.

- Focus on *you, we* and *us*.

- Don't change your blog's domain address; it's easy to lose your audience this way.

- Tell the truth.

- Read lots of blogs.

- Link liberally to other blogs. Your post can include an excerpt from the other blog in quotation marks, but don't include more than a paragraph or two—more than that could get you accused of copyright violation.

- Link to your previous posts.

- Don't be boring. Ruffle some feathers. A good blog takes sides.

- Don't rant on side issues outside your blog's focus. Your audience will tire of this quickly.

- Break news.

- Be authentic. In the blog world, this is known as "keeping it real."

- Tell stories. Have a conversation.

- Vary your sentence length. Frequently.

Blog to e-mail Service

Loyal readership is key to your blog's success, so make it easy for first-time visitors to keep reading. One of the simplest ways for readers to receive your blog posts is by e-mail subscription.

FeedBlitz.com operates a popular blog-to-e-mail service. It provides a snippet of code you can insert on your blog to display a sign-up box or button where readers can provide their e-mail address. Subscribers receive an e-mail digest of any new blog posts, and can click through to your site to read more.

A subscription service makes it more likely that readers will stay with you because they won't need to remember to return to your Web site. An e-mail service is a simple solution for your readers who might not understand how to use Bloglines or other newsreaders.

Only about 20 percent of blog readers understand newsreaders, so if you're not using e-mail, you're missing 80 percent of your potential audience.

The two best alternatives to FeedBlitz are Aweber.com and MailChimp.com. Of all three services, MailChimp is perhaps the easiest to get started with, and it offers the most generous free trial program, so you can put the service through its paces without paying a dime.

E-mail services also provide you with a valuable business asset. You'll have access to those readers directly, so you can send special messages for events like publication dates and book tours. This is why many bloggers encourage readers to sign up for e-mail delivery: It provides an automatic marketing channel for special messages about you and your book, without having to manually collect contact information by some other means.

The blog-to-e-mail services provide a fully automated double opt-in process, so there's no danger of your blog posts or occasional promotional messages being mistaken for spam.

Search Engine Optimization

The beauty of publishing a blog is that it makes your writing easy for folks to find. A blog makes you highly visible, without your having to think too much about technique. Even so, it helps to know some basics of search engine optimization (SEO) to enhance your site's ability to draw new visitors.

The essential ingredients for a high-ranking site change periodically. Many bloggers and webmasters waste time and money chasing the "perfect" formula for getting to the top of search results, and then must start over when Google changes the way it evaluates Web pages. Rather than spending lots of time trying to game the system, you can better spend your time adding valuable content to your site.

Keyword Density

One effective way to make your content more visible with search engines is *keyword density*. Let's imagine you're writing a blog post about how to wax a car in 30 minutes. You might write the title: "Waxing your car in less than 30 minutes: Here's how." This way, the most important words, *waxing* and *car*, appear at the beginning of the title. Your first sentence might be, "Waxing your car can be a time-consuming chore, but here's how to get it done fast." This reinforces your keywords. Repeating them again will enhance your keyword density and ensure your post ranks high in searches for those keywords.

Be consistent with word choices to maintain keyword density. Let's imagine you have a page on your site devoted to antique Ford Thunderbird cars. Naturally, you'll want *Thunderbird* to appear several times on the page to rank high in search results for that keyword. So you'll want to keep using the word *Thunderbird* instead of slang or nicknames. The sentence "The 1969 '*Bird* was a stylish car" would dilute your keyword density.

Although keyword density makes it easier for your target audience to find you, don't overdo it. If you artificially jam the same keyword several times in each sentence, search engines will detect this and penalize you for "keyword stuffing."

Another way to get penalized by search engines is by participating in so-called "link farms." These are sites that trade or sell Web links, but it seldom works. The only links that will truly boost your site are from high-ranking sites with content similar to yours. So forget about buying links to boost your SEO. Simply produce good content for your audience, and the links and traffic will come naturally.

You've probably seen advertisements for consultants who promise to make your site No. 1 in the search engines within 30 days. Don't waste your money. Chances are, anyone who makes such promises is incompetent, a charlatan, or both.

Your most important links will be from sites in your niche. Links from crowded social sites like Facebook or MySpace or discussion boards won't strengthen your site's rankings much, says Dave Taylor, author of *Growing Your Business with Google*. "Theoretically, all links are good, but I don't believe that links from jungles like MySpace are going to give you any real boost," Taylor says. "Those sites that are easy to get links from just aren't going to have the value of, say, a link from the home page of Stanford.edu or Wiley.com."

Google provides an excellent tutorial for optimizing your Web site, including a Starter Guide for absolute beginners:

http://www.google.com/webmasters/docs/search-engine-optimization-starter-guide.pdf

Syndicating Your Blog Content to Other Sites

Besides offering your blog content via e-mail subscriptions, you can also export your blog content to other social sites like Facebook and your author page at Amazon.com. Since you're putting some effort into creating this content, you'll want new readers to be able to discover it in as many ways as possible. Wherever you have a web presence, announce your other web presences.

QR Codes are those square black and white boxes with a lot of dots and mysterious-looking patterns that are used for storing addresses and URLs (Uniform Resource Locators). The QR stands for Quick Response. They may appear in magazines, on signs, on buses, on business cards, or on almost any object—like a label or a book cover—about which users might need information.

 People with a camera phone equipped with the correct reader application can scan the image of the QR Code to display text, contact information, connect to a wireless network, or open a web page in the telephone's browser.

Once you have all of your online presences in place, you can generate your own QR code to direct customers to where they can find you online—probably your website, which has links on it to everything else, especially your online store where they can purchase your books.

You don't need a QR code, but bear in mind that the people who are reading your eBooks and are interested in all that is quick and convenient will appreciate having one available. And it makes you look all high tech and savvy when you have one prominently displayed on your site, in your e-mail signature, and/or on those old fashioned business cards of yours that you hand out at weddings and book signings.

It's easy to generate a QR code, and once you have it, you can save the file (like a picture) and put it wherever you want to; several sites offer to do so free online. Here are a couple:

http://www.qrstuff.com/index.html

http://qrcode.kaywa.com

Blog Tours

So far, we've explored techniques for luring readers to your blog or Web site. Now we'll turn to outreach campaigns—going where part of your potential readership already congregates.

You can introduce your book to lots more readers with a series of appearances on blogs catering to your audience—a *blog tour*. Sometimes it's called *guest blogging* or a *virtual book tour*.

Blog tours are especially valuable for authors unable to travel, uncomfortable with public speaking, or whose dispersed audience makes touring impractical. Blog tours can expose your book to a much larger audience than a traditional bookstore tour, while requiring less time and money. Blog tours are especially helpful in launching new books.

"Blogs are like rocket fuel for online book publicity," said Steve O'Keefe, executive director of Patron Saint Productions, a book publicity firm.

Blog tours are also a good deal for the host blogger, who gets free content for his or her readers and affiliate revenue from book sales.

Typical blog tours include these elements:

- A book excerpt or "guest post" displayed on the host blog to publicize the tour appearance. The excerpt might be part of a book chapter, an article, or a favorite blog post.

- A one-day appearance, beginning with an opening statement or a short essay on the topic of your book. Then the floor is open for discussion.

- Follow-up visits for the next four to seven days to answer questions and comments from blog readers.

Targeting Host Blogs

Your first step in arranging a blog tour is finding potential host blogs. Start with those that you have already built a relationship with by following. Then, add the most popular blogs read by your book's target audience. Some likely candidates may spring to mind, but new blogs can gain readership quickly, so it's worth surveying the field periodically.

Once you've identified a list of potential blog hosts, prioritize them by three criteria: activity level, reader involvement, and traffic volume.

- **Activity level:** How frequently do new posts appear on the blog? Usually, bloggers must post new content a few times a week to sustain a loyal readership. Scan the past few months of blog archives to determine the posting frequency.

- **Reader involvement:** How often do readers chime in with thoughtful comments? The vast majority of blogs allow readers to follow up with their own commentary. The frequency and thoughtfulness of reader comments indicates audience engagement.

- **Traffic volume:** Traffic is the natural result of audience loyalty and involvement, and it's an objective measure of a blog's impact.

Measuring Blogs at Alexa.com

A handy yardstick for measuring blog traffic is www.Alexa.com, which provides estimated traffic reports on many Web sites. Enter the Web address of the blogs you're considering at Alexa.com to access traffic rankings and the most common keywords readers use to find the site. You can also discover links related to the given website and sites that link to it. (Alexa's data is also a handy tool for keeping track of your competitors.)

Depending on how narrowly focused your book is, you may find only a few relevant quality blogs, and that's fine. It's better to focus on a small, well-qualified audience who will respond to your book instead of a general audience where you'll have little impact.

Alexa's reports aren't foolproof; they're drawn from a small sample of Web users who use its browser toolbar. Rankings for high-traffic sites are more statistically accurate than reports for niche sites. In any case, Alexa is a handy, free source of objective information about Web traffic, and it is more accurate than anecdotal reports. Bloggers and Webmasters are notorious for overestimating their traffic.

Alexa, which is a subsidiary of Amazon.com, isn't limited to blogs, so you can use it to find all sorts of Web sites targeting your niche.

Other good free sources of Web metrics are Compete.com and Klout.com, which enable you to compare your influence over multiple sites.

Your Pitch to Bloggers

Okay, you've got your excerpt (or guest post) ready, and you've compiled a list of prospective blogs for your tour. It's time to pitch your book to the host bloggers. Contact each blogger individually by e-mail or the contact form at their website, explaining why your book is of interest. Provide two or three compelling reasons why your tour will be thought-provoking and entertaining for *this blog's audience.*

Start with your top prospects and work your way down as time permits. Contact bloggers directly; don't simply leave a comment on their blog and hope they notice it. Most blogs have a mechanism for contacting the blogger through an e-mail address or contact form.

Sometimes, the more popular a blogger is, the harder it is to get their attention. If you can't find contact information, look at the bottom of the home page, where you may see instructions for contacting the "Webmaster." An "advertise with us" link may sometimes be the most reliable way of reaching a decision-maker.

Tailor your pitch for each blogger, addressing them by name, otherwise your message can be mistaken for spam. Offer a complimentary review copy of your book. Provide your complete contact information including phone number, which also differentiates your message from spam. The subject line of your e-mail must be specific; a generic "Please read this" often is deleted unread.

The excerpt includes everything the blogger needs to decide whether to approve your tour appearance. If approved, a copy of the excerpt can be posted at the host blog to promote your appearance in the days preceding the tour.

A Sample Pitch

Here's a sample script for pitching your blog tour:

SUBJECT: Author [NAME] as guest on [BLOG NAME]

Dear [BLOGGER NAME]

I'm a regular reader of your blog and believe it's one of the best sites about [TOPIC]. I'm writing to see if you would consider having me as a guest on your blog on Monday, May 9, to discuss my book, [TITLE].

I believe my book is of particular interest to your readership. [REASONS, BRIEFLY]

I'm hoping to have a dialog with your readers. If you approve, I'll take a day on your blog, make an opening statement, and respond to comments as long as they keep coming.

I hope you'll give this a try. Below my signature, I've provide the text I'd like to use for my appearance.

I'd also like to send a complimentary review copy of the book. Just let me know where to mail it.

Thanks for your consideration,

[SIGNATURE]

[POSTAL ADDRESS]

[PHONE NUMBER]

Not every blogger will accept your pitch, and you shouldn't take the rejections personally—an acceptance rate of 25 percent is a good target. Some sites simply don't use book excerpts or guest posts.

As realistically as possible, pitch yourself as a potential long-term partner, not a drive-by opportunist. Successful blog tours will prompt return invitations and can launch a mutually beneficial relationship.

Earning Side Income From Your Blog or Site

A steady audience on your Web site provides additional income opportunities through affiliate programs and advertising. If your site becomes extremely popular, the revenue could rival your income from book sales.

Some bloggers report that a combination of affiliate and advertising revenue can result in about 1.5 cents of income for each unique daily visitor to your site. At that rate, a site averaging 1,500 unique daily visitors can generate about $8,200 in annual revenue—not bad for something that requires no ongoing work on your part. Depending on your audience and the type of products related to your book, you might do better or worse.

New sites usually generate negligible revenue, but advertising or affiliate programs can still be worthwhile. Your audience may appreciate niche advertising, and these programs can boost your visibility with search engines. One option is to donate your affiliate and ad revenues to charities admired by your audience, which sometimes can be handled automatically. The public-relations benefit of donating could outweigh the monetary value, and you won't have to account for it as income and pay tax on it.

In any case, advertising shouldn't overly distract visitors from the main purpose of your site—generating awareness of your book.

Here are some of the leading advertising and affiliate programs authors can use on their Web sites:

Amazon Associates Program: Amazon's affiliate program is called Amazon Associates. After joining, you can display special links on your blog or website for your book and related books and products on Amazon, and when your visitors click through to Amazon and make a purchase, you're paid a commission. Amazon Associates is one of the most familiar and successful programs on the Internet, with more than 1 million member sites. It is not available in all states, however. There are separate programs for each territory Amazon operates in—the United States, Canada, the United Kingdom, France, Germany and China.

Under Amazon Associates' performance-based compensation plan, affiliates earn referral fees ranging from 4 percent to 8.5 percent, depending on volume. For a site referring 21 or more affiliate sales during a quarterly period, Amazon awards 6 percent, payable at the end of the quarter. You can collect your fees in the form of a check, direct deposit, or an Amazon gift certificate.

Besides providing Amazon Associates links to specific books, you can display a variety of Amazon banner ads or search boxes on your site, and you'll earn referral fees on sales resulting from those clicks.

In 2006, Amazon Associates introduced a new contextual program called Omakase, which displays different products based on the content on your site and your visitor's browsing history at Amazon. The advantage for affiliates is that Omakase is dynamic, exposing your audience to different books each time they visit a different page on your site, increasing the odds of a purchase.

The name Omakase is Japanese for "Leave it up to us," a custom in Japanese restaurants in which the chef improvises a meal based on his knowledge of the diner's preferences.

For more information, visit:

https://affiliate-program.amazon.com

Barnes & Noble's affiliate program isn't as widely used as Amazon's but it can attract buyers who prefer Barnes & Noble, particularly members of its loyalty program. Members receive an additional 10 percent discount on purchases. For more information, see:

http://affiliates.barnesandnoble.com

Google's AdSense program is perhaps the best-known Web ad network, and it's relatively easy to sign up and incorporate text or banner ads onto your site. For more information, see:

www.google.com/adsense

Project Wonderful is another popular ad network. For newer blogs and websites, they are smaller and a bit easier to navigate than Google AdSense. Also, they tend to pay a bit quicker. For more information, see:

http://www.projectwonderful.com

Generating buzz on Social Media

Social media can produce grassroots buzz that helps sell your book. Nowadays the king of social media is Facebook. In just its first few years, Facebook has grown from a college dorm-room project to one of the most popular Internet destinations. The site is the second most frequently visited website, attracting millions of visitors each month. And, while Google currently ranks No. 1 in visitors, Facebook far outranks it in the amount of time spent using it. It has become the dominant force in a phenomenon it helped to create: online social networking.

Facebook appeals to a fundamental human need: connecting with other people. At its basic level, that is what social networking is all about. Facebook has become ubiquitous because it helps us make and keep connections. For example:

- Some of your best memories of high school involve playing on the varsity volleyball team. But somehow, over the years, you have lost touch with all your teammates. Facebook can help you reconnect.

- You move to a new city where you don't know a soul. That experience can be exhilarating but it can also be a little scary. Facebook can help you find people who share your interests.

- Your friends from college are spread out all over the country. You would like to keep them informed about what's going on in your life, and you would also like to know what's happening in theirs. Facebook is like an online class reunion—without the last-minute dieting.

- You've decided to launch a home-based business. You expect that your first customers will be friends, family and acquaintances. Facebook gives you a convenient way to tell everyone you know (and their friends) about your new venture.

It helps that Facebook is easy and fun to use. Signing up takes just a minute or so. Once you have signed up, you can easily search for friends or join an online community. You can also use Facebook to promote yourself or your book. That is the focus of this book.

But before we look at using Facebook for promoting your book, let's see how this phenomenon started and where it seems to be heading.

In the beginning...

In 2003, Harvard sophomore Mark Zuckerberg embarked on a fairly sophomoric project. He hacked into Harvard's computer network and downloaded student identification photos of many of his fellow students. Then he placed two photos next to each other on a website and asked users to choose the "hotter" person. He called his site "Facemash."

The site became an instant hit on campus, but Harvard administrators were unhappy with Zuckerberg's project. They accused him of copyright violations, security breaches, and invading students' privacy. He even faced expulsion, but eventually the school dropped the charges. The next semester Zuckerberg launched "The Facebook," a photo directory of Harvard students. Within a month, half the student body had become members.

Colleges had been publishing "face books" of their students, especially freshmen, for years, but Zuckerberg was the first to put it all online. At first, access to the site was restricted to Harvard students, but in 2004 The Facebook expanded to include Stanford, Columbia and Yale. The expansion continued rapidly, and by 2005 membership was open to students at most U.S. and Canadian universities.

With membership growing exponentially, Zuckerberg moved his base of operations to Palo Alto, Calif., and bought the domain name "facebook.com" for $200,000. In 2005, Facebook opened membership to high school students, and by 2006, membership was open to anyone over the age of 13 with a valid e-mail address. Today the site claims to have over 845 million active monthly users worldwide.

Who's on Facebook? Since Facebook started on a college campus, many people assume that it is mainly for young people. While it is true that 70 percent of U.S. users are 25 or younger, the percentage of users in the 35+ age group is still growing. Almost 72 percent of all U.S. Internet users are now on Facebook; worldwide, the number is one in every 13 people on earth, with over 250 million of them (that's more than 50 percent) who log on every day.

In the U.S., more women than men use Facebook, but beyond that, it's hard to pin down the demographics of Facebook members. For example, there is no data available on the ethnicity, income or politics of the entire Facebook membership. If, however, you decide to buy ads on Facebook, you can target your ads by age, gender, location, education and other variables.

In terms of promoting yourself or your book, the important thing to realize is that membership in Facebook is so huge that you will probably have no trouble finding a large target audience.

Getting Started with Facebook

If you're just using Facebook to promote yourself or your book, you don't necessarily need a personal account. But having your own Facebook account is a good idea for a couple of reasons. First, it helps you learn what Facebook is all about. The overwhelming majority of Facebook users are individuals, not businesses. Having a personal account lets you see what the Facebook experience is like for the people you want to reach.

Second, Facebook is fun. Just because you want to use Facebook for promotional purposes, that doesn't mean you can't enjoy all the other cool things it offers, such as keeping in touch with relatives, sharing photos, and telling all your friends about your latest amazing achievements.

If you're already intimately familiar with Facebook and are ready to begin applying it to your business, you might wish to skip directly to Chapter 7, Facebook Pages, and Chapter 10, Paid Advertising on Facebook.

Signing Up for Facebook

Joining Facebook is fast and easy. All you need is a valid e-mail address (an address that allows you to send and receive e-mail). Begin by going to Facebook.com. Fill in the information in these boxes:

- **Full Name:** Use your real full name. Do not use a phony name or alias. Facebook has controls in place to protect your privacy.
- **Your E-mail:** Enter the address where you would like to receive e-mail.
- **Password:** Choose a password that is easy to remember but not obvious. Some people suggest using a password that is unique to Facebook and not one you use everywhere else.
- **Select Sex:** Choose male or female.
- **Birthday:** Enter your birth date. You can hide this information if you want.

After you've entered this information, Facebook will congratulate you and tell you that a message confirming your registration has been sent to your e-mail address. Go to your e-mail, open this message, and click on the link. You will be taken to Facebook's "Getting Started" page.

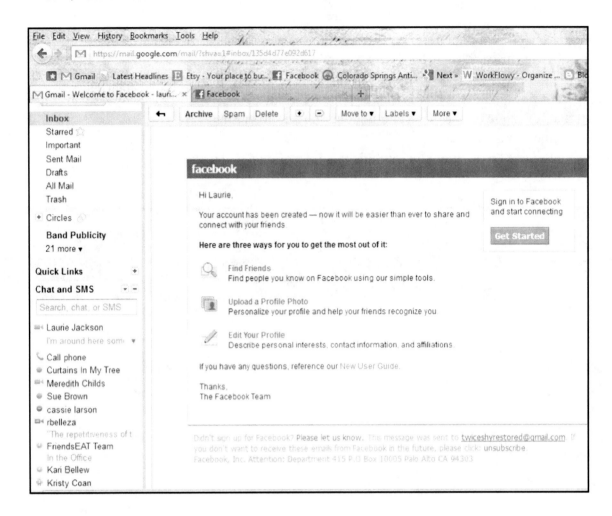

The Getting Started Page

The purpose of the Getting Started page is to find people you know who are already using Facebook. You can enter your e-mail address book and let Facebook tell you which of your contacts are on Facebook. You can also look up friends individually by entering their name in a Search field. You can skip this step if you like.

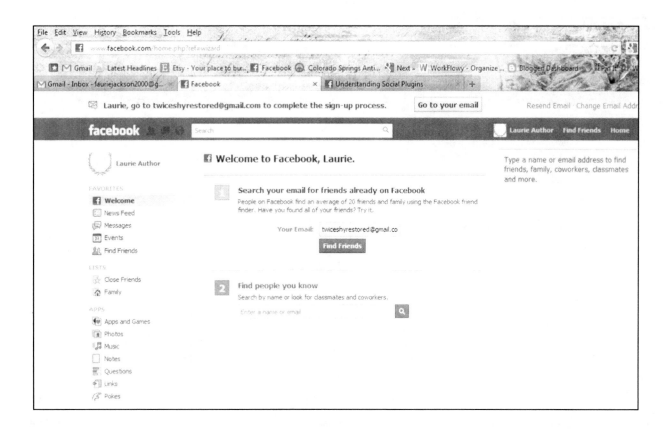

View and Edit Your Profile

This is your chance to tell the world as much (or as little) about yourself as you choose. At the top of the screen you can click on a box called Edit Profile. Here are some of the kinds of information you might choose to let people see:

- Current city
- Hometown
- Sex
- Birthday
- Whether you are interested in women or men
- Languages spoken
- About me—a place to type in any other written information you would like to be included in your profile

If you're using Facebook mainly to promote yourself or your book, you should give some thought to what kinds of information you want to include in your personal profile. For example, there is no reason to alienate potential readers or fans by informing the world that you belong to a particular political or religious group—unless your purpose is to network with folks belonging to that group. If you decide later to remove some information from your profile, just click "Edit Information" and delete whatever you like.

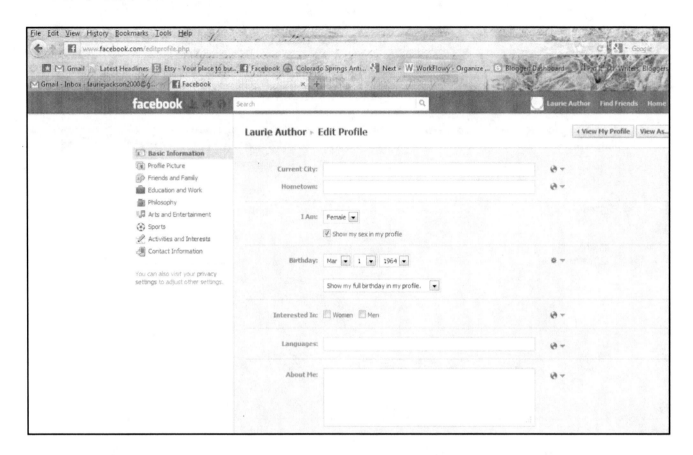

Add a Profile Picture. Facebook is all about faces. Your profile picture becomes an essential part of your online identity. People see your profile picture when they search for you, and your friends see it when they click on your profile. Many people choose a candid shot rather than a posed photo for their profile picture, probably because candid shots are usually more interesting. They give people a better sense of who you are.

Facebook accepts most common types of digital photos. To add a profile picture, click on the silhouette on the top left of your profile page. You will be asked to either upload a photo from your computer or to use your computer's webcam to add a photo. You can change your profile picture at any time by clicking on it and following the directions. Now you can include even more information by clicking "Info" on the left side of the page.

The first section is called Work and Education. Click on the pencil icon and the word Edit next to it and you may then fill in the name of your employer, where you went to college, and where you went to high school. Facebook likes everyone to add this basic information to their accounts, and you will notice that unless/until you do, you will see a prompt at the top of your page asking you to add it!

The second section is called Arts and Entertainment. Here you may click on the different icons to enter information about music, books, movies, TV shows, and games.

The third section is called Basic Information. Here is where the personal information you already entered under Profile will show up.

Finally there is a section called Contact Information, where you may provide additional phone numbers, instant messaging screen names, your physical address, and the addresses of other places you can be found on the web.

Facebook Pages

A Facebook Page is like a free website. It doesn't give you the flexibility of a website in terms of appearance, but it is an effective way to create a presence on the web at no cost. You can use your page to tell people about your book, and to announce upcoming events, such as book signings and other public appearances. If you have a blog, here is another place you can publish your blog posts. You can also promote your blog on your Facebook Page, and vice versa.

Facebook Pages are profiles of a business and in this case, your book. They're easy to create and they're free. Just click "Create a Page" at the bottom of any Facebook screen or "Pages" on the left of your home page. You will be guided through the process of setting up your page when you click on "Create a Page."

1. **Select a category and name for your page.** Click on "Entertainment" and you see a category for books. The name of your page should be the exact name of your book.

2. **Add a profile picture.** Choose a picture that will look good even when it is shown as a thumbnail. Book covers often don't fit the space for the profile picture, so you may want to create some type of art work and then crop it to the correct size. '

3. **Add a cover photo.** Again, your book cover will not match the dimensions of this space so you might want to get creative here. If you book is about organic strawberries, here's an opportunity for a photo of strawberries. You can post a cover of your book, but remember that you are not allowed to say anything about how to buy it or offer a discount on your cover photo.

4. **Add information.** Tell people all about your book. The more information you add, the better. Think about the questions that your potential readers are likely to have. What do they care about? What's important to them? If your book is about a famous person in history, post some interesting facts. Did you know that there are more than a dozen varieties of strawberries?

5. **Make it captivating.** What keeps you on a given page for any length of time? It all comes down to interesting content. Add as many engaging photos as you can find. Use video if you have it. One of your goals is to build a community of loyal customers. Every aspect of your page should reinforce the idea of community.

6. **Publish your page.** Tell all your friends and readers about your page and ask them to tell their friends. Remember that connections on Facebook are exponential, or what some people call "viral." Each of your Facebook friends has friends, and those people have friends, and on and on.

7. **Keep your page current.** Add news, comments and announcements frequently. Using new photos is an easy and effective way to freshen up your page.

Promoting Your Book on Facebook

Facebook offers three ways to promote your books. Perhaps you already have a personal Facebook account. If you don't, it's easy to create one and, once you've done so, you can then create a page for your book or perhaps a single "author" page where you'll promote all your books.

While a Facebook Page is similar to a personal profile, unlike a profile, it is oriented to businesses and products. As a bonus, Facebook gives Pages detailed insights about how people view and interact with your content.

A Facebook Page is a great tool for creating interest in your book, but only if you make it interesting for people to read.

Here are some other ways you can use a Facebook page to promote your book:

- Post short excerpts

- Show off your cover or other art

- Highlight different editions of your book, and what makes each unique

- Publicize special offers, such as Kindle sales or other limited time offers in your newsfeed

- Link to favorable reviews or other media mentions

- Keep a calendar of events such as book signings and speaking engagements

- Create buzz about your book by linking it to current events

The author of a book about making handmade gifts can post on Facebook in advance of each gift-giving holiday, reminding everyone that an occasion is approaching and suggesting they pick up your book for gift ideas. Health and fitness authors can link to web content that is in agreement with or related to their book's subject or point of view—or not. Anyone who writes about politics or technology has ample opportunities—probably daily—to reinforce their book's ideas or update their readers.

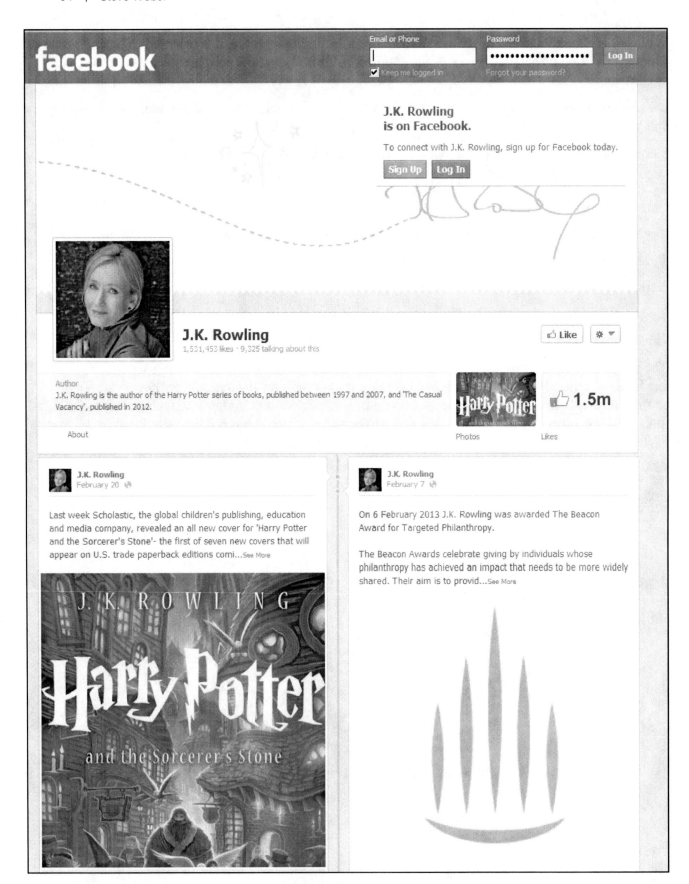

Whatever you have written your book about, you are already plugged into that subject and the communities associated with it—or you should be. If your book is about whales and a Great White washed up on the shore in Europe somewhere, put a link to news stories you find online about the plight of the animal on your Facebook page. In these ways, you are sparking interest on topics related to your book in your book's target audience. It also helps to establish you as kind of an expert in the field you have written about, or if not exactly an expert, at least as someone who is up on the current news and information on the subject both you and the reader are interested in.

You can also post tips or short informational tidbits from your book. One author of a how-to book on communicating with your ex, posted a chapter, two or three sentences at a time, delivered every six to ten days over the course of a year. She also reposted any inspirational quotations and relevant articles she found on other Facebook pages.

Facebook offers two main vehicles to promote your book and yourself:

• A Facebook Page, which is like a personal profile with a few important differences. Unlike a profile, it gives you detailed insights about how people view and interact with your content.

• Facebook Ads, which take the concept of targeting specific audiences to a new level. You can define the audience for your ads by age, education, gender, interests and other variables. You can even tell people what their friends think of your products.

Seven Ways to Use Facebook to Promote Your Book

Here are some examples of using Facebook to promote your book. Although the following suggestions are in no particular order, we'll illustrate them throughout this book. After you have had a chance to experiment a little with Facebook, you will probably come with your own brilliant ideas on how to use it to promote your book.

Create a personal profile. You don't need to create a personal profile to advertise on Facebook, but if you don't, you won't have a real understanding of what Facebook is all about. You can't make the most of Facebook as a promotional tool if you don't understand how people use it.

Join a group. Groups are meeting places for people who share common interests and offer some interesting marketing possibilities. Suppose you have written a book about Agatha Christie. You could join one (or more) of the 99 Facebook groups devoted to the famous mystery writer.

The first step in joining a group is choosing one from among the thousands of groups available. Just type in a few key words in the search bar at the top of any Facebook page and see what turns up. For example, if you type "Agatha Christie," you will get a list of all the places on Facebook devoted to that prolific author. You can then click on the Search Filter in the left sidebar, Groups. (If you don't narrow the search to Groups, you can tell which are Groups rather than Pages because there will be a bar to the left that says "Join Group" rather than "Like.")

The Groups that are open to be joined will say "Open Group" below the name. If it says "Closed Group," you will need to be invited by a member.

Explore a few of the groups that your search turns up to see which ones might be worth joining. You can check out most groups without joining them just by clicking on the name of the group. In particular check out the discussions to see if they are worth reading. If you like what you see and the group is open, just click "Join This Group." You can also be added to a group by a friend who is already a member. And you may be swayed to join the group with the most members.

On the group's home page, you will find:

- Basic information about the group
- List of members (click on About next to the name of the group at the top of the page)
- Discussion board
- Wall much like your own wall on Facebook
- Photos
- Links

Every group has a discussion board. If you find a group whose members are indeed among your book's target audience, you can eavesdrop on these discussions as a sort of basic market research tool. You can also join the discussion and let people know, in a low-key way, who you are and what your book offers. Don't make your contribution to the discussion sound like an ad. People join groups to share information and opinions, not to be bombarded with ads.

A few words of caution: First, if you contribute to a discussion, your contribution should actually have some relation to the shared interests of the group. For example, don't start talking about your Agatha Christie book on the discussion board of a group devoted to the Pittsburgh Steelers. The administrator of the group may delete your post, and other members of the group will probably be angry about your irrelevant comments.

Even if your contribution to a discussion is relevant, you don't want it to sound too much like an advertisement. With a little creativity, you should be able to write something that sounds more like an announcement than a commercial.

Keep in mind that when you join a group, its members cannot see any more of your information than they would otherwise. In other words, if you have privacy setting on your profile set to "Friends Only," group members who aren't your Friends won't be able to access your information.

Start your own group. If you can't find a group that is really relevant to your book, you can create your own group and recruit your friends and loyal readers to become members. Here's how:

From your home page, go to the Groups section on the left side menu and click on "Add Group." Click "Create New Group." A pop-up box will appear where you'll be able to add a group name, add members and select the privacy setting for your group. Click the "Create" button when you're finished.

Once the group is created, you will be taken to the group's page. To get started, click at the top right of the page and select "Edit Group Settings." From here you can add a group description, set a group e-mail address, add a group picture and manage members.

You'll need to provide some basic information about your group including:

Name: Think of something catchy (or at least descriptive).

Members: You will need to indicate which people you want to add to the group.

Privacy: The options are "Open," "Closed" and "Secret." Open means anyone can see the group, who's in it, and what the members post. With Closed, anyone can see the group and who's in it, but only members see posts. Only members can see Secret groups, who's in them, and what members post.

When you start a group, you automatically become its administrator. You can then appoint other administrators at your discretion. Administrators have control over the group's content and membership.

When you establish a group, you can invite your Facebook friends to join it. If you decide to make membership open to anyone on Facebook (most groups are), then other people can join if they're interested.

Your group page will appear in the left hand column of your home page, under the heading "Groups." When you click on it, you will be taken to the Group's page and from there you can write a post, add Photo/Video, ask a question or upload a file, just like you can on your own personal page. Members may also do these same things.

Besides providing free exposure, groups can also give you valuable information about what people think of a particular topic or in this case, books—either yours or your competitors' books. By spending some time on the discussion board in a group, you can get a good sense of what people love or hate about whatever you are trying to promote.

An easy way to do this is by using the Ask Question option at the top of the Group page. Click on Ask Question and you will see a box that says "Ask Something." Just type in your question, such as, "What is the name of the last book that you bought, and where did you buy it?" You can add options you have already thought of, and also give your group members the option of adding their own option/answer. As readers answer the question, their responses appear next to the question.

If you decide that running your group is more trouble than it is worth, you can just delete it. You might have to delete all of its members first, and then leave the group before it is deleted. On the other hand, you might decide that groups offer a fairly easy way of building a community of people who are interested in what you would like to promote.

Once you've created your first group, it is easy to create more, as you will then have a filter on the left of your home page called "Groups" and an icon to click on that says, "Create a Group!"

Sponsor an event. Sponsoring an event can be a worthwhile promotional activity, even if you don't use the Events feature on Facebook to publicize it. Small businesses sponsor all sorts of events: fund raisers for nonprofit organizations, instructional workshops for customers, open houses. Events like these get your name in front of the public and attract people to your book. By using the Events feature on Facebook, you can announce your event to a wider audience and keep a record of who plans to attend.

Whenever you are having an event related to your book, like a book signing or a speaking engagement, you will want to publicize the event by creating an Event on Facebook. It's one more way to get the word out, and by using the "Event" feature, you can announce your event to a wider audience and keep a record of who plans to attend.

When you create an event, it shows up on your Facebook page and those who visit your page can click on the event to learn about it.

Update your customers. Use your Facebook page to send updates to your fans about anything new that is happening with your book. Did it win an award? Get reviewed in a publication? Post about it on your Facebook pages and share links. You can also send updates to people who like your page via personal messages on Facebook; just be careful to reserve those kinds of updates for big events or special occasions. If fans get tired of seeing your updates, they can easily block them.

Buy ads. Advertising on Facebook offers several advantages. You can easily define a target audience by age, gender, location and interests. You can mount an ad campaign on a very modest budget, and you can set a limit on how much you will spend on advertising each day. You can see detailed reports on how people are responding to your ads. And finally, you can add a "social" element to your ads that will allow people to see if their friends have become fans of your book.

Keep connected. If you have a website, you know that the best way to keep people coming back is to give them something new to look at. The same is true for Facebook. If you have a Facebook page, post on your wall frequently. Use the events section of your page to let people know what you have coming up. Send updates to your fans whenever you have something interesting to announce. If you belong to a group, contribute to the discussion board frequently, and pay attention to what other people are saying. If you have a personal profile, keep connected with your friends. That's what Facebook is really all about.

Facebook Ads

Advertising has become so pervasive that it's nearly lost its effectiveness. The more often people are bombarded with ads, the more they tend to tune out the messages. But targeted advertising can be effective, especially for a product like a book.

The most effective ads put information about a product or a service right in front of you at just the right time, almost as if marketers were reading your mind. That is the basic strategy behind Google's advertising. When you perform a search, Google shows you ads directly related to the topic you're looking for. Google's e-mail program, Gmail, searches your incoming messages and shows you ads related to key words in the text.

With Facebook, you can target your ads precisely by age, gender, location and many other variables. When you create your ad, you can decide if you want it to direct people to your own website, to a Facebook page, or to some other location on Facebook, such as a Groups or Events page.

The unique thing about Facebook ads is their "social action." When someone is shown your ad, Facebook shows them how many of their friends have interacted with your Page. For example, your ad might say, "Visit our restaurant today! Your friend Betty Blue lLikes it."

With a Facebook ad, you will receive regular reports on your ad's performance (how many people have seen it, how many have clicked on it, etc.). You will also receive useful demographic information to help you ensure that you are reaching the right audience.

More social media opportunities

Pinterest and Twitter are two good examples of social media sites, although they're completely different—one is visual and one is verbal text. Depending on the type of book you have, you might want to use one or both to augment your Facebook presence. Each attract a different audience. So far, Pinterest has caught on with women, many of who are interested in crafty, food and home-related photos. Twitter is big with politicians, journalists, Hollywood stars, and others who like its short, almost abbreviated messages.

Pinterest is a virtual pin board, or inspiration board—a place online to store photos of all of the interesting things you find as you surf the web. How can you use pinterest to promote your books? Here are some ideas:

First, remember that Pinterest strives to be a social media community, and they are just beginning to make strides to get users to see it as such. And just as with other social media sites, you need to create a community or a following first. Once you register on the site, take a few moments to write a biography and upload a photo to represent you. Feel free to mention your book and/or direct people to your author website in your bio: it's allowed.

Next, search for boards curated by other users with whom you have something in common, and follow them in the hopes that they will follow you in return. Once you start adding followers and boards to your account, do some exploring among their boards to establish even more contacts.

At the same time, begin to create boards for your own account that will draw in followers. A couple of no brainers would be to pin a board full of books that are similar to yours. Feel free to create a separate board just for your book onto which you pin a photo of the book's cover from your Amazon page, and content from all of your book's other online presences.

Next, create more interest in your own book by creating some boards for it. Let's say for example your book is a non-fiction a travel guide for Hawaii. Create a board with photos of that island's best beaches, reviews of resorts, and things worthy of sightseeing—especially things you've mentioned in your book.

What if your book is fiction? Then create a board for each of your book's main characters. Find online content that related to your character. For example, if your character was a famous chef with a penchant for pesto, you could post recipes for dishes made with that sauce that you imagine she would have liked onto her board. Did she collect kaleidoscopes? Find some lovely examples online and pin them. Do this for each of your characters, and let your imagination run wild. Do you have pets featured in your book? Make a board for each of them and post examples of their breed to the board. Make a board for your book's setting or location and pin examples of destination photos on it. Anything that might spark interest in any aspect of your book is fair game. After all, the point of pinterest is to inspire.

Twitter

The subject of using Twitter to publicize your own book almost requires its own separate tome. Suffice to say, the consensus on Twitter is that it takes time to establish your credibility/following on Twitter and it might not be the best way to create book buzz. Which is to say, we are all still learning how to use it to promote books. Twitter seems to work best for personalities that are already well known—or at least known to you. The average person is bound to pay more attention to tweets from their wife or Ashton Kutcher than to tweets from aspiring authors.

The key to success in Twitter marketing is investing the necessary time to interact with other Twitter users. Only when you become part of the conversation and show that your contribution is helpful to others will people begin to pay attention to your tweets.

If your book is non-fiction, Twitter is a great way to get the attention of journalists who might want to use you as a source, reference or expert on your subject. But again, unless you already have contact with these followers, there may be other ways to spend your time and energy.

The best way in which Twitter can help you sell your book is when customers who buy it on Amazon (or add it to their wish list) click on the little icon to share their purchase/wish on Twitter.

LibraryThing

www.LibraryThing.com was launched in 2005, and like other social sites, part of the fun is belonging to a big club that lets you display how eclectic and singular your taste is. Meanwhile there's the chance you'll meet a few one-in-a-million literary soulmates who are passionate about the same books as you.

Spending time on LibraryThing is addictive because of all the interesting connections that surface, especially with obscure books. Entering your copy of Harry Potter won't move the needle. But when you enter your copy of *Environmental Kuznet Curves*, things get interesting.

Members enter their book collection simply by punching in the ISBNs. Then members can compare their whole collection—or individual rarities—against the collections of others. Ever wonder who else in the world has read that oddball book you love? On LibraryThing you'll know.

LibraryThing also has a book recommendation system that founder Tim Spalding claims is more accurate than Amazon's, simply because its users pay more attention. On LibraryThing, members input the books they want to drive their recommendations, no matter when or where they acquired them. Books you've purchased as gifts easily corrupt Amazon recommendations, and most users don't input the books they've purchased elsewhere.

Further, Amazon recommends only current books available through wholesalers, the ones it can sell. Since LibraryThing isn't a bookseller, it's free to recommend out-of-print books. Finally, LibraryThing recommendations are filtered, drawn from the collections of other users like you, not the whole universe. Harry Potter isn't recommended to everyone.

Another difference is LibraryThing's anonymity. Unlike a bookselling site, which must identify users to collect payments, LibraryThing knows only a user's log-on name—unless that member posts more information and makes it public. This gives members the freedom to list books and provide other information they'd rather not be associated with publicly.

As an author, you can build a special page on LibraryThing to show members what's on your bookshelf. To become a LibraryThing author, you must have at least one book listed at Amazon or the Library of Congress, and you or another member must add the book to LibraryThing. Also, you must catalog at least 50 books on LibraryThing, and you'll need a public account that allows comments on your profile. Get more details by sending e-mail to Abby@LibraryThing.com.

Whether LibraryThing will generate the same kind of demand for niche books as commercial networks like Amazon is unclear. But the potential for such user-generated recommendations is huge. The bookselling network www.AbeBooks.com, which sells new and out-of-print books, bought 40 percent of LibraryThing in 2006. AbeBooks will use LibraryThing's data to provide book recommendations to customers.

Goodreads

Goodreads.com, another social site dedicated to books, came along after LibraryThing and has eclipsed them in membership and popularity. Amazon purchased Goodreads in 2013.

For authors, one attraction of Goodreads is that it helps authors find readers who might be inclined to post a review to Amazon or Goodreads itself. The site's "giveaway" program allows authors to provide complimentary review copies to readers who request copies:

http://www.goodreads.com/author/program

When you sign up for the Goodreads Author Program, you generate a profile page which can include a photo and biography, a list of your own favorite books, the option to sync your own blog to Goodreads, and more ways to interact with readers. Once your Goodreads page is established, you can add all your books to it. You can also measure the traction you're getting on Goodreads by viewing how many people add your book and mark it "to-read."

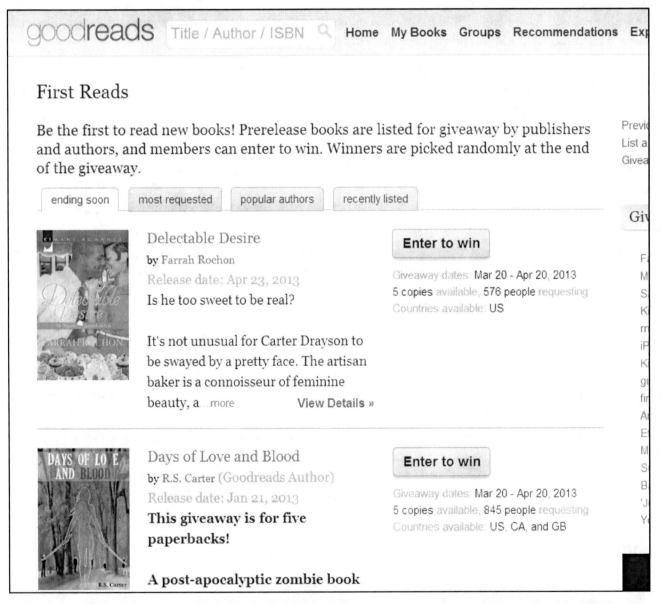

The benefit of doing your giveaway through Goodreads is the built in, specific audience. In other words, you will be giving your book away to someone who truly wants to read it—not someone who might have just googled "free giveaway" looking to get something (anything) for nothing!

The biggest benefit of becoming a Goodreads Author is to rack up reviews for your book. When you give away all those books, ask the recipients if they will agree to read and review them on the site. Similar to Shelfari, when a Goodreads member publishes a review of your book, it is shared with their friends and they are also able to post their reviews to Facebook and Twitter.

The key to getting Goodreads to work for you is to invest a bit of time in interacting on panels and on any of the wide variety of forums available on the site, and with other members interested in your genre. This is a way to establish relationships with readers and other writers, share information, and perhaps even learn something yourself.

Click on the "Explore" tab at the top right of the Goodreads page and take a look around. You can check out their membership—who has written the most reviews, read the most—even who is online right at the same moment you are. It is one of the better online communities for readers—and writers!

Digital Media's Level Playing Field

He's often derided as a hack, a second-rate talent, an obnoxious huckster. But Joe Konrath has laughed all the way to the bank, raking in $1 million in royalties since 2009 from his mystery, thriller and horror books.

Despite his success, Joe is better known for how his books are published, rather than the books themselves. And Amazon's Kindle figures prominently in this story.

After leaving Chicago's Columbia College in 1992, Joe spent the next dozen years writing nine manuscripts and collecting 500 rejections for them. His 10th book was the charm. Whisky Sour was picked up by Hyperion, launching his series featuring Lieutenant Jacqueline "Jack" Daniels of the Chicago Police Department.

But Joe was irked. He still couldn't find a publisher for his first nine books. Not Hyperion, not anybody.

So, rather than watch his manuscripts collect dust for another dozen years, he published them himself using Amazon's Kindle self-publishing website. That's when he really started selling books, and folks in the literary world finally noticed him. But a lot of them didn't like what they were seeing.

Traditions die hard. Hundreds of authors and agents railed against Konrath's insistence on publishing his own work, arguing that no professional stoops to self-publication. Period, end of story. As author Mike Cane put it, "Well, it seems Konrath is still smarting over novels one to nine and is still shocked they weren't good enough."

To counter his critics, Konrath started a blog, A Newbie's Guide to Publishing, where he dispenses advice to fledgling writers.

To distill Konrath's advice to three sentences, it's this: Authors must take responsibility for their own success or failure. Don't wait for someone else to champion your book because the odds are, nobody will. So once you've polished your manuscript, get off your duff, rattle some cages, and bang on enough doors until it's published—or do it yourself. And perhaps most important of all, eBooks and the Kindle give authors direct access to readers.

It's hard to argue with Konrath's results. Instead of making a nickel or two for each of the mass-market paperbacks his publisher might sell, he's made a dollar or two for each Kindle book. And instead of selling a measly 10,000 – 20,000 paperbacks like before, he's moved hundreds of thousands via Kindle. And he's done it with the same manuscripts every traditional publisher in the country left in their slush pile.

Joe is still at it, writing and publishing more books on the Kindle and in paperback using Amazon's CreateSpace service. Lots of people love his books, and some people simply can't stand him. But Joe isn't really worried.

"There will always be people who don't like you, and don't like your books," Konrath says. "Ignore them. Trust me, it is liberating to be free of the opinions of strangers."

Make no mistake, the eBook and self-publishing have arrived. Amazon recently announced that John Locke, a crime novel writer, became the eighth author to sell more than 1 million of his books on Kindle, and he's the first self-published (also known as "indie") author to do so. Locke has some good company in the "Kindle Million Club," including Stieg Larsson, James Patterson, Nora Roberts, Charlaine Harris, Lee Child, Suzanne Collins and Michael Connelly.

It's no secret that eBooks are currently the most profitable and fastest growing sector of publishing, but it might surprise you to know just how quickly the market is growing. Today, 28 percent of Americans use an eReader such as a Kindle, iPad or Nook, up from 15 percent in 2011. The average Kindle user buys 3.1 times as many books as they did the year before. Ebooks saw triple-digit percentage growth from October 2010 to October 2011, but print sales declined again, leading to an overall drop in trade book sales of 7.8 percent.

Konrath, of course, is only the tip of the iceberg. Consider Amanda Hocking, who had self-published the Trylle trilogy and six additional novels by age 28 thanks to the Kindle. So far she's sold more than 1 million copies of her books, mostly via the Kindle, and is considered the exemplar of self-publishing success in the digital age. When you find that type of success on your own, opportunities start coming out of the woodwork. After her success with the Kindle, Hocking landed a traditional publishing contract for paper copies of her book with St. Martin's Press.

The relative ease and speed of self-publishing eBooks has revolutionized the publishing industry. Authors no longer have to wait in line for their books to be chosen by an old-school gatekeeper like an agent or an editor. With Kindle publishing, you can hire your own editor, and upload your finished book directly to Amazon, and earn royalties as high as 70 percent.

Part of the reason for the success of eBooks is Amazon's dedication to investing in their Kindle product–even to the point of losing money. This pays off in the long run with future and repeat sales once a customer acquires a Kindle. With the growth in sales of iPads and Nooks, and the availability of the Kindle App for other devices, which allows people to read on their smartphones, eBook sales have exploded and will continue to grow.

Kindle Direct Publishing Select

One of the ways that Amazon helps to you to publicize your Kindle editions is by allowing you to participate in a program called KDP Select. If you agree to distribute your eBook exclusively through Amazon for a period of 90 days, Amazon will offer your ebook to customers on loan as part of their Lending Library. With this exclusivity (and they do check!), you commit to make the digital format of that book available exclusively through KDP. During the period of exclusivity, you cannot distribute your book digitally anywhere else, including on your website, blogs, etc. However, you can continue to distribute your book in physical format, or in any format other than digital.

Perhaps the most important publicity tool KDP offers authors is the ability to offer your book as a temporary free download to Amazon customers in their Lending Library. This is a collection of books that Amazon Prime members who own a Kindle can borrow once a month with no due dates.

With KDP, your books will still be available for anyone to buy in the Kindle Store, and you'll continue to earn royalties from those sales like you do today. The exact amount you'll earn for each time someone borrows your book varies from month to month, but it averages about $1.75.

Some authors report that the temporary free promotions result in a big boost in paid sales after the free promotion ends.

For more information on KDP Select, see:

https://kdp.amazon.com/self-publishing/KDPSelect

Google Books

The Google Books program allows publishers to make previews of their books available on the Web, much like Amazon's Look Inside the Book program. If you wish, Google also will sell eBook editions of your work at its online bookstore and through its app store for Android device users, https://play.google.com/store/books.

For more information about making your books available through Google, see this page:

http://books.google.com/intl/en/googlebooks/publishers.html

Google Books provides free worldwide exposure for books, which is particularly valuable for publishers of niche and backlist titles where an expensive marketing program isn't feasible, according to Jennifer Grant, product marketing manager for Google Books. "That's really where Google and technology can come into play and help market these books very cost-efficiently ... and help these books find their readers."

For much of its history, Google Books served readers through its website, www.books.google.com. More recently, with the growing popularity of smartphones and tablet computers, more readers have accessed this resource through the "Books" section on the Google Play app store, https://play.google.com/store/books.

Multimedia for Books

As high-speed Internet service becomes more common, audio and video content are becoming valuable tools for online book promotion. Multimedia is particularly effective for niche authors and newcomers who haven't attracted mainstream media coverage.

Multimedia grabs the attention of younger people who spend more leisure time online, while consuming less traditional media like newspapers and television. Meanwhile, production and distribution of trailers is getting easier and cheaper by the day, thanks to inexpensive video cameras and free hosting sites like www.YouTube.com.

Book "trailers," which often resemble movie previews, music videos or talk shows, are an increasingly popular tool for book publicity. Even though trailers are promotional materials, the people who choose to watch often perceive them as interesting, valuable content.

Remember Amanda Hocking, the wunderkind of digital bookselling success? She has created trailers for each of her books which are available to view on her website. But better than that, these short videos are often featured in front of any interview she gives online, providing a way to grab potential audiences in a new and different way—visually.

For authors and publishers, trailers can serve as an infomercial, a message that appears on a cable network of 5 million channels—except you have global reach and very low costs. The videos contain a "buy this book" link to Amazon or the publisher's site, prompting impulse purchases from viewers, which can make an effective trailer instantly profitable.

Creating a trailer isn't much more difficult than putting together a PowerPoint presentation. It begins with writing a script. You then need to decide on the visual content—photos, videos, music—and then put it all together with some editing software, like Apple's iMovie or the widely available Windows Movie Maker. Be sure to use only content you have permission to use otherwise you won't be able to share the video on YouTube for free.

Once your trailer is complete, upload it to YouTube and then start sharing it by linking to it from all of your online presences. You can also promote the video by sending it out in much the same way you would a written press release.

Producing a book trailer does take some skill, knowledge and patience. If you don't think you'd be able to do a great job yourself, consider hiring a specialist to do it for you.

Podcasting for Publicity

Podcasts are yet another way to connect with readers in an audio format. Folks can listen to podcasts on their PCs, or download them to a portable music player such as an iPod. The word podcast is a combination of the word iPod and broadcasting, but no iPod is required—anyone with speakers on their computer can listen. A podcast is somewhat like an archived radio program freely available for on-demand listening. Books are sometimes serialized in podcast format, sometimes referred to as a "podiobook."

If you have existing audio recordings of interviews or book-readings, you might be able to repurpose them as a podcast. Or you might do a "live" interview with a recurring podcast. There are hundreds of podcasts about books, writing, publishing and virtually any topic area in fiction and nonfiction.

The most popular directory of podcasts is available through iTunes, which can be installed on PCs, Macs and other devices. For more information, see:

http://www.apple.com/itunes/podcasts/specs.html#submitandfeeback

A free alternative to iTunes is Micro Guide, available at:

http://www.getmiro.com/publish/guide/

Let's take a look at how one new author, Scott Sigler, embraced podcasting and gave his writing career a fantastic boost. After years of writing, Sigler had nothing to show for it except a stack of rejection slips. Then Sigler heard about "podcasting," a kind of Internet radio. He started recording episodes from his book, *EarthCore,* using a microphone plugged into his computer. He recorded the episodes in his apartment's walk-in closet, standing between the hanging shirts to muffle street noise.

Word spread, and every week thousands more listeners downloaded the free episodes to their computer, iPod, or portable music player. By the time he was finished, Sigler had 30,000 listeners, a literary agent, and a hardcover bestseller. Since then, Sigler has scored two more bestselling books, and Random House is selling audiobook versions for $34.95. Nobody seems to mind that anyone can already listen to, read or print the stories from Sigler's Web site. In fact, the exposure just brings more fans to Sigler, fueling more word of mouth, more sales.

Nonfiction authors have succeeded with podcasting, too, perhaps none better than Mignon Fogarty, host of *Grammar Girl.* She got the idea for a show about grammar tips because, from years of editing, she had lots of advice to give. She made a new podcast every week, although sometimes the recording was interrupted when her upstairs neighbors started doing the laundry.

Fogarty's five-minute grammar lessons were a nice blend of useful advice and entertainment. Her weekly audience quickly swelled to 100,000. Suddenly, she got a book contract from Holt and was invited to appear on The Oprah Winfrey Show. Because the show aired before she finished writing, Fogarty cobbled together an audiobook using existing material she planned for the book.

After her appearance, the audiobook topped the chart on iTunes, the Apple music and audio store. By the time Grammar Girl's Quick and Dirty Tips for Better Writing was in paperback, there was a built-in audience, making it a reference bestseller. Steady exposure from the podcast has fueled continued sales.

Just like blog-reading provides insights for building your own blog, listening to podcasts will inspire ideas for producing your own audio content. Here are some directories where you can sample what's available:

- iTunes: www.Apple.com/itunes/podcasts. Here you can sample or subscribe to podcasts.

- PodioBooks: http://podiobooks.com/. Serialized audiobooks.

- LibriVox: Librivox.org. Free audiobooks from the public domain.

To record material for your podcasts, all that's required is a microphone and PC. Free software for recording and editing podcasts is offered at www.Audacity.Sourceforge.ne and also at Wavosaur.com. If you're an Apple user, check out "Garage Band," part of the iLife software package on OSX.

Networked Books

Traditional books have always been published into a finite form. When the author, editor and proofreaders finish their part, the die is cast—unless the book was one of the relatively few popular enough to survive for another edition. No wonder they're called "dead-tree" books.

With the advent of eBooks, a book can remain fluid and open to new facts and contributors.

A networked book is a relatively new phenomenon. When books and people are connected, they come to life. One of the best things you can do for your readers and yourself is to simply print your e-mail address in your book's introduction. Ask for reader comments, suggestions, and corrections. In return, you'll get a gold mine of ideas for new editions, books, and spinoffs. A networked book doesn't require a flashy Web site or a big name. The mere suggestion that you're open to ideas from readers inspires their loyalty.

Author John Locke recently networked in an unusual way with his loyal readers. When he was trying to decide whether or not he should publish a backstory about one of his popular characters, he posted a brief synopsis of it and some of his concerns about it (it was dark) and asked readers to comment. Within 24 hours he had received more than 500 comments from readers who wanted to contribute their advice.

When authors connect in this personal way with their readers, they strengthen that relationship which results in loyalty and word of mouth.

Interactive eBooks.

eBooks have an elemental form of interactivity, enabling readers to search for content, highlight words, record notes, view dictionary entries of words, or adjust the font size and other display properties. The next generation of eBooks promises more, such as easy integration of video, audio, and two-way communication between readers and authors. These are the truly interactive books of the future—a kind of current version of the children's pop-up book, only smarter. Student texts in particular offer great possibilities. Books might be able to self-narrate the text and offer periodic self-testing to gauge student progress.

Interactive books are valuable whenever they enhance the experience of the reader by enriching the content or enhancing the reading experience in a way that wasn't possible with paper books. For example, if you can refer to a genealogy chart while reading a book that spans a family's generations, to remind yourself of a character who appeared earlier in the book, it enhances the book. Providing easy access to a specialized glossary or timeline in a historical book enhances its value.

One of the most impressive examples of a truly interactive book is *London: A City Through Time*, which covers 2,000 years of that city's history for iPad users. Packed with facts, maps, and sightseeing recommendations, it's more valuable than a tour book and more visually stimulating than a coffee table book. It boasts 6,000 articles on the capital's museums, statues, buildings, streets, trades, people, parks, rivers and more, with 2,000 images of rare prints and photographs. The book has 35 video clips. Panoramic views of the city at various stages throughout its history can be viewed as high-definition, zoomable images, plus 360-degree views of the capital's grandest sites, plus artifacts from the Museum of London, are included. There's even an underground subway guide to let you know what's above ground, stop by stop.

Apple, the maker of the iPad, offers a free program for composing interactive books called iBooks Author, available here:

http://www.apple.com/ibooks-author/

Audiobooks: If you've ever wished your book was available in audiobook format by a professional narrator but didn't know where to begin, try the Audiobook Creation Exchange operated by Amazon at www.acx.com. Using this service, you decide how your audiobook is produced, who narrates it, and where it will be sold (choices include Amazon, Audible.com, and iTunes). If you own the audio rights to your book, you can register your book at ACX and begin the project by posting some sample text and auditioning some narrators.

Once you've found a narrator, you make an offer/negotiate a deal (price, timeframe, etc.) using a form that ACX provides online. You have a few options for ways to pay the producer, including a one-time fee for production or a royalty sharing option. Depending upon which option you choose, you stand to earn 50 percent to 90 percent royalties on gross sales if ACX is the exclusive distributor, and from 25 percent to 70 percent if ACX is not the exclusive distributor. The share of royalties you earn increases as the quantity of your sales rises.

Completing your audiobook project might take anywhere from four to eight weeks, depending on its length and the schedule of your narrator. Once the recording project is complete and available for sale, you'll receive monthly statements and royalty payments from ACX.

Advanced Amazon tools

While advertising is rarely a cost-effective marketing technique for books, online *paid placement* can be a useful tactic if it delivers your message to your target audience and delivers results. Since Amazon has such a large share of book buyers, it offers some of the best opportunities for showcasing your book.

Buy X, Get Y

You can increase the odds of buyers finding your book by paying at least $750 a month to display it with a complementary book in Amazon's Buy X, Get Y program, known as BXGY. The primary benefit is your book's cover is prominently displayed on the detail page of a related book under the heading Best Value. Customers who buy both books get an additional 5 percent discount.

Before we go any further in discussing BXGY, you should understand that Amazon makes the program available only in certain circumstances. First, larger publishers can participate if they pay Amazon many thousands of dollars per year in marketing fees, known as "co-op" payments. Books from smaller publishers can qualify if the book is sold through "Amazon Advantage," a self-service consignment program, but many publishers find its terms unfavorable. For more information about Advantage, see:

www.amazon.com/advantage

You'll pay more for a pairing with popular books. Amazon charges $1,000 a month for pairing with a book with a sales rank of 1 to 250, and $750 a month for pairing with slower-selling books.

An ideal BXGY campaign would pair your title with Amazon's No. 1 bestseller, so long as that bestseller appealed precisely to your audience. The stronger the Amazon Sales Rank of the paired title, the more people will see your promotion, and the more traffic will be redirected to your book's detail page. But if the paired title isn't relevant to your book, it won't work. Pairing your book with the latest installment of *Harry Potter* would bring a ton of exposure, but it wouldn't produce many sales, unless your book was aimed at the same readers.

You can find BXGY candidates by browsing Amazon's category bestseller lists; here's where to begin:

www.amazon.com/Best-Sellers/zgbs

To find more suitable books for pairing, search Amazon's book section for relevant keywords. Use the "Sort by" drop-down menu on the right to sift the books according to popularity (sales rank), publication date, and price. After browsing the search results, use Amazon's "Look Inside the Book" feature to get more information about the content of the titles.

Some publishers have tried pairing two of their own titles for BXGY, figuring it would boost sales of both books, but this seldom works. The main value of BXGY is sending readers to your book's detail page, which they might not find it otherwise. You can pair your title with only one other title at a time.

Weaknesses of BXGY

Amazon doesn't provide any figures on the success rates of BXGY promotions. Anecdotally, many publishers complain that while the program increases sales a bit, the revenue from those increased sales rarely covers the fees. However, BXGY is a tool some publishers use to spark initial word of mouth for a book, and in that sense it can be considered an investment. As discussed previously, increasing your sales on Amazon often leads to more success, bringing years of steady sales.

Often BXGY offers aren't compelling for buyers. Customers don't qualify for the program's 5 percent discount unless they purchase both the books new from Amazon; purchases of used copies don't count. For this reason, pairing your title with an older classic isn't effective if there's a plentiful supply of used or discounted copies. Buyers don't have much incentive to buy both books at full retail when they can get one deeply discounted.

Amazon offers more paid placement programs to large publishers, who can buy spots on Amazon's home page, category pages, and in specialized stores and seasonal lists such as "Back to School" or "Top Cookbooks of 2013." However, these placements aren't available to smaller vendors or self publishers.

Free Paired Placement

Okay, we've learned that BXGY is tricky to join and horribly expensive. Now, for the good news: you can get BXGY-like exposure without paying fees if your book sales are strong, relative to other titles in your category. Amazon pairs your book with a related title in a display nearly identical to BXGY's Best Value, but in this case it's called Frequently Bought Together.

To see this in action, go to any book's detail page on Amazon. Under the heading Frequently Bought Together, you'll see the book paired with three more books, much like BXGY, albeit without the extra 5 percent discount.

If your book is the best-selling title in its niche, your book can appear on the Frequently Bought Together spot for several other related titles—another example of how strong sales on Amazon create more exposure for you.

Listmania!

Listmania! lists allow any Amazon user—readers, authors, music-lovers, movie buffs—to create lists of their favorite items organized by theme. Listmanias appear in various places on Amazon, like product detail pages and alongside search results. Listmanias that mention your book can expose your title to thousands of potential readers on Amazon, and can even appear in Google search results.

Listmanias are ranked by popularity among shoppers, based on viewership and the number of votes calling it "helpful." For example, one popular list is dedicated to novelist Nick Hornby and was compiled by one of his fans. Under each novel is a pithy quote from the Listmania author, just enough to convey the gist of each book and why it appears.

The list includes most of Hornby's books, other books Hornby edited or wrote introductions for, and a few other novels by writers with similar styles. See this list at:

www.Amazon.com/gp/richpub/listmania/fullview/1X1GGDBXARHZ6

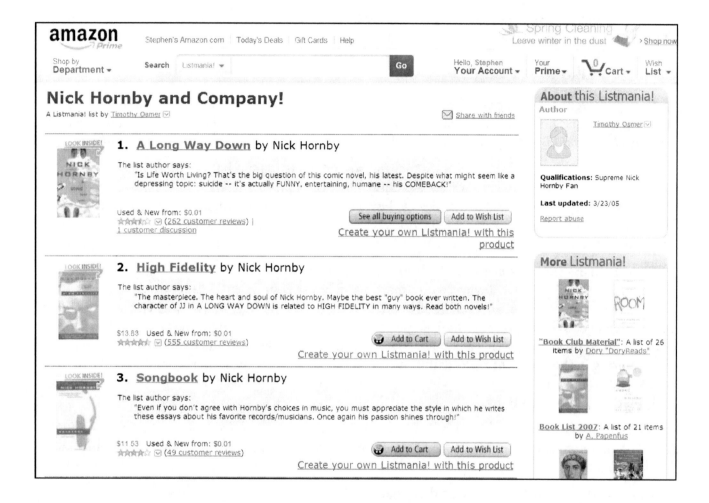

As an author, you're free to recommend books yourself with a Listmania! list, mentioning up to 25 books in your list.

Niche books stand to gain the most from Listmanias. The more focused a Listmania is, the more helpful it is to buyers hungry for specific information—so the more likely it is to be noticed, read carefully, and acted on. Niche Listmanias have less competition—Amazon can show only so many "Harry Potter" Listmanias while the thousands of similar lists wait in a queue. But your Listmania about "Organic Strawberries" may pop up in front of every single customer looking for a relevant book.

To write a Listmania:

1. Visit your Profile page at www.Amazon.com/gp/pdp.

2. Click the "Edit Your Profile" button on the top right-hand corner of the page.

3. Click the "Lists" tab in the Contributions section of Your Profile.

4. Click the "Create your first one now" link or "Manage your Listmania Lists" link if you already have existing lists.

5. Provide the requested information for your list and click the Preview button to review your list and Publish list when you are finished.

Your Listmania! list will appear on your Profile and in search results related to items on your list. From your Profile, you'll have the option of editing your lists or deleting them.

So You'd Like to . . . Guides

Have you ever wished you could submit a how-to essay to your local newspaper that demonstrates your expertise and helps publicize your book? You can accomplish much the same feat on Amazon by writing a *So You'd Like to ...* guide, which could be read by more people than a newspaper article.

Amazon's *So You'd Like to ...* guides somewhat resemble Listmania! but are more like tutorials. They're time-consuming and require considerably more original writing than Listmanias, but are consulted often, especially in niche topics. A short excerpt from your book might serve as the basis of a guide. And for your trouble, you get to insert your book's cover image and a link so readers can buy it at Amazon.

For example, when I wrote the first edition of *Plug Your Book*, I published a related So You'd Like to... guide titled, "Get Your Book Reviewed on Amazon and Boost Your Sales." I did it partly to share my tips, and partly to see how effective it might be in publicizing this book. Boy, was it ever! Not a week goes by when I don't get a thank-you note from someone who read the guide, bought the book, and took time to e-mail their thanks. Because it's a popular topic posted on a trusted website, the search engines love it, too, resulting in thousands of clicks daily. Search on Google for "get Amazon reviews" and it's the first result. That is the kind of organic exposure nobody can buy, at any price. Share some of your own ideas, and you can do the same thing.

To include your book or other merchandise in your guide you'll need to look up the 10-digit ASIN (Amazon Standard Identification Number) that appears on the item's detail page under the heading Product Details.

To get started writing a guide, visit this page:

www.amazon.com/gp/richpub/syltguides/create

Click on "Create a guide." As you compose your guide, insert book ISBNs wherever you want to refer to a book in this format:

<ASIN: 1234567890>

You should use the characters "ASIN" even if you're using a book ISBN. Don't enter the book title, because Amazon will take care of that automatically.

Guides must include at least three ISBNs or ASINs and may have a maximum of 50. The first three ISBNs/ASINs you mention in your guide will become featured items that appear at the top of your guide when it appears on Amazon.com.

Break up your guide into sections every few paragraphs by inserting a subheading like this:

<HEADLINE: (Type your headline here)>

Before finishing, copy your text into a word processor and spell-check it. After you're finished writing and editing your guide, click on the Publish button.

Later you can add books or revise your guide any time by visiting your profile at www.Amazon.com/gp/pdp. In the middle of the page is a heading for "Contributions." On the right tab, click "Guides" and you'll see a list of your published guides.

Look Inside

If you strolled into your local bookstore, and all the books were shrink-wrapped shut, would you be inclined to spend much time shopping? Probably not. Looking at a book's chapters, reading a few sentences, and seeing if there's an index are part of the buying process. Yet Amazon operated with this "closed book" handicap for its first eight years—customers couldn't actually see inside the books.

In 2003 Amazon enrolled the first 120,000 books in Look Inside (sometimes called *Look Inside the Book*), enabling buyers to view sample pages and search the complete text, providing millions more ways for buyers to stumble onto your book.

Previously, buyers could search only for words in book titles. With Look Inside, anyone searching for words contained somewhere in your book can find it, even without knowing the title or author name. For example, if a shopper searches Amazon for *Eleanor Rigby*, the top three results are books whose titles contain Eleanor Rigby. Then come another 568 books that mention Eleanor Rigby on at least one page.

Like nearly every Amazon innovation, Look Inside was resisted by many publishers, who insisted it would hurt book sales. Why, they argued, would anyone buy a book—especially cookbooks, travel guides, or other references—if they could view the pages they wanted without paying a dime? But after Amazon reported average sales boosts of 9 percent for titles enrolled in Look Inside, most publishers signed up.

Amazon uses Look Inside to sell books just like Baskin-Robbins sells ice cream: by giving people a sample right when they're in a position to buy, says Amazon chief executive Jeff Bezos:

> "If you went to the middle of Central Park on a hot day and let people sample your ice cream, they *might* come back later [to your store] and buy some. But if you let them sample ice cream right next to the cash register—inside the Baskin-Robbins—you're definitely going to increase sales. So the idea is to literally let people look inside the book and find what they're looking for."

Bezos concedes Look Inside doesn't convert everyone into a buyer. Many people use it as a research tool without paying, but were probably not likely buyers anyway.

Amazon builds safeguards into Look Inside to prevent customers from reading large portions of a book without buying it. Users must register with a credit card first, and can view no more than 20 percent of any particular book. The text displayed on the screen is a low-resolution image, and it can't be copied into a word processor or easily printed.

Look Inside also provides a unique marketing opportunity for crafty writers able to hook readers with their first sentence. Amazon displays your initial sentence hyperlinked, so interested readers can click straight through to your whole introduction. If your book has a long first sentence, only its first 125 characters are displayed on the detail page, followed by an ellipsis.

To enroll in Look Inside, go to:

www.amazon.com/gp/help/customer/display.html?nodeId=14061791

Writing Book Reviews

For nonfiction writers, half your battle is establishing a reputation as a thought leader in your field. One way to build your reputation is by writing reviews of books by other authors in your field. Writing a compelling review of a popular book can enhance your reputation and expose your name to many more readers.

Don't hype your own book or mention its title in your review of other books. This is viewed by many as blatant self-promotion, and it can result in your review being deleted by Amazon. However, many authors add their book titles to their Amazon pen names displayed with reviews, such as "John Steinbeck, author of 'The Grapes of Wrath." To change the way your name is displayed, go to your Amazon Profile at www.Amazon.com/gp/pdp. In the top right corner, click the "Edit my profile" button. Use the "edit name" and "edit signature" links to make your desired changes.

To write a review, from the book's detail page on Amazon, scroll down the left column below the three "most helpful" reviews, and click the button for "Write a customer review."

A good review focuses on the book's content, including whether you liked or disliked a book, and why. The maximum length of reviews is 1,000 words and the recommended length is 75 to 300 words. The title of your review is limited to 60 characters.

Amazon strongly discourages the following elements in customer reviews:

- Spoiling a story's ending or revealing crucial plot elements

- Dates of promotional tours or lectures that become outdated

- Commenting on previous reviews of the book (other reviews might be edited or deleted in the future)

- Profanity or cruel remarks

- Single-word reviews

- Contact information such as phone numbers, addresses or URLs

- Discussing the book's price, availability, or shipping information

- Asking people to "vote" for your review

Check your review for spelling and typos by running the text through a word processor. Break up your text with a blank line between each paragraph to add white space.

Reviews usually appear on the website immediately, but can sometimes take a few days to process.

The more helpful your review is to Amazon users, the more often it will be voted "helpful" and have an impact. Of course, the "most helpful" reviews have the most impact since they appear prominently. Your review has a better chance of becoming a "most helpful" review if it's published soon after the book's publication date. Once a review receives several "helpful" votes from other customers and is highlighted on the site, it becomes increasingly rare that a subsequent review can garner enough votes to knock it from its perch. Be honest in your reviews. As a practical matter, though, it's best to avoid reviewing books similar to yours from competing authors. In fact, Amazon asks you not to. Enormous feuds result from negative reviews posted on Amazon by competitors, and your time and energy can be better spent improving your own work.

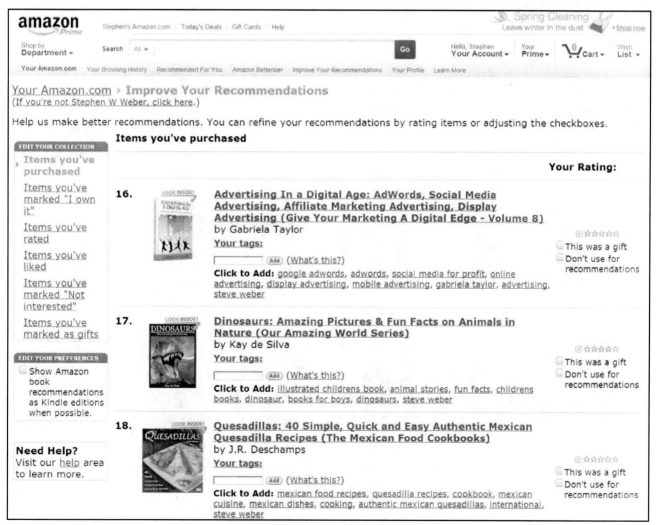

Fine-Tuning Book Recommendations

Because so many sales can result from Amazon recommendations, it's worth spending a few minutes looking under the hood—it will help you visualize one more way for readers to find you.

From your Profile's top navigation bar at www.Amazon.com/gp/pdp, click "Improve your recommendations."

You'll see a list of the books and other items you've purchased, with the most recent on top. You can refine your recommendations by rating items (one through five stars, just like a book review) or adjusting the checkboxes (indicate whether to exclude the item from recommendations, perhaps because it was a gift). The star ratings you assign to books on this list won't be visible to other Amazon users, but the ratings can affect which books get recommended to whom and how often.

Customers new to Amazon can benefit more from the "Amazon Betterizer" page, www.amazon.com/gp/betterizer. When a visitor arrives at this page, they're shown six items each from books, movies and music and are asked to click a "Like" button for those of interest. For items not of interest, hover over the picture until you see an option to select "Not interested."

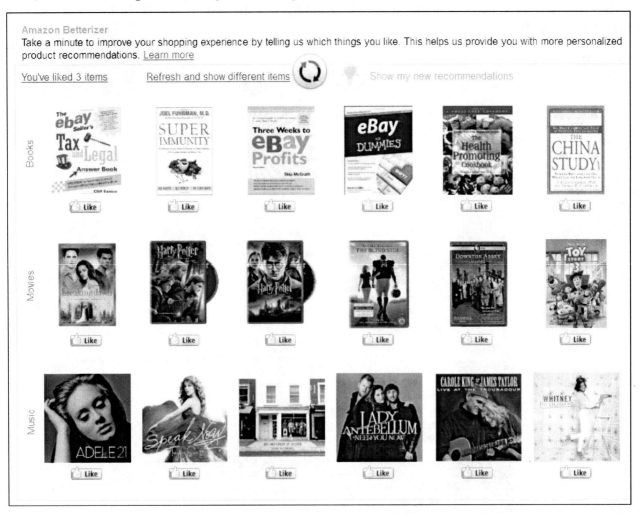

The display is refreshed with more personalized recommendations, and similar items are displayed as the customer navigates the website. Recommendations also have a dedicated page in each customer's account at the "Your Store" page, www.amazon.com/gp/yourstore.

Few Amazon customers take the time to confirm this raw data in Amazon's recommendations engine, and as a result it can spit out some wacky suggestions. If you've purchased books for children or friends that you wouldn't read yourself—and you haven't taken the time to exclude these items from your recommendations—the result is faulty recommendations. Fortunately, in some cases, Amazon will guess correctly which of your purchases are gifts—for example, when you ship a book to a different address—and excludes them from recommendations.

Here's how to exclude other inappropriate books from your recommendations:

- Underneath the Featured Recommendations in each category of "Your Amazon.com" page, you can click on the right facing arrow to "See all recommendations in Books." In the blue bar at the top of the page is the phrase, These items are based upon items you own and more."

- Clicking the link "you own" shows the list of books Amazon knows you've purchased.

To refine your recommendations, indicate whether you'd like to exclude the item from your recommendations. Here you can also assign a star rating and/or add tags for each item in your purchase history.

Amazon Bestseller Campaigns

The Internet has become an effective marketing tool for authors because it enables your audience members to find *you*, instead of you finding *them*. With online word of mouth, you gently reel your audience in, instead of blasting an advertisement to a crowd that isn't listening.

Let's face it, traditional advertising is dying, and it never worked with books anyway. More than ever, people are tuning out commercials, junk mail and spam.

There is no shortcut for getting word of mouth for your book. And as we'll see, not only are shortcuts ineffective, they can backfire.

One shortcut many new authors are trying these days is "Amazon Bestseller Campaigns." And who can blame them: What author doesn't want to have a No. 1 book and millions of loyal readers?

Amazon doesn't endorse these campaigns, but doesn't really discourage them either. Independent marketing consultants charge $2,700 for their Bestseller Campaign courses, and to a new author it might seem worth every penny. According to advertisements by these Bestseller consultants, one author racked up more than $35,000 in book sales during the first 48 hours of her campaign. Could it happen to you? You bet—you'll have a "guaranteed" bestseller within "38 days."

So go ahead, dream a little. Once your book tops the chart at Amazon, you'll be on the red carpet. Lunch with publishers. Bookstore tours. Agents calling. Movie deals, foreign rights sales. And next, you'll be on the *real* bestseller lists: *New York Times, USA Today*, and *Wall Street Journal*.

So what's wrong with all that? The bestseller consultants say they're simply applying good old-fashioned marketing to the digital age. But critics say these campaigns are just smoke and mirrors. These consultants don't discuss whether the book needs to be any good. Apparently anyone who coughs up $2,700 is guaranteed a bestseller.

Is it too good to be true? Are these programs worth it, or just a waste of time and money?

Let's boil it down to three essential questions:

1. Are Amazon Bestseller Campaigns profitable? Do they generate more income for the author or publisher than they cost?

2. Do these campaigns enhance the reputation of the author and the book?

3. Most importantly, does the bestseller promotion provide enduring word of mouth for the book, or do sales evaporate quickly?

Making the List

We're list-crazy these days. Everything is ranked: books, movies, radio and TV shows, Web sites, video games. The lists are dutifully reported in newspapers and magazines and many even get mentioned on news broadcasts. Who's No. 1 today? Who's up and who's down? How many gazillion dollars did the latest Hollywood blockbuster rake in last weekend?

Actually, this stuff matters a lot: Most of your sales happen *after* you're on a list, because that's how lots of people discover you. For years, big publishers have used every trick in the book to break onto lists like the *New York Times* Best Sellers. One way is to offer huge discounts to certain retailers who place big orders, making demand appear strong.

For struggling authors, Amazon is the most democratic list because *everyone* gets on it, whether they sell tons of books or just a few. Each author who has sold at least one copy of his or her book on Amazon is ranked somewhere in their catalog. The top dog has an Amazon Sales Rank of #1 and is racking up thousands of sales a day. The worst laggard is ranked 3,500,000-plus, selling perhaps one copy every few years.

Just for kicks, plenty of authors buy a copy or two of their book on Amazon, just to watch their Sales Rank spike a few thousand notches higher toward No. 1. But your Sales Rank slides right back down unless someone else buys another copy pretty soon.

Whether an author is No. 5 or No. 539,000, many simply can't resist checking their rank several times a day. And since Amazon's bestseller list is recalculated hourly based on the preceding hour's sales, the list changes 24 times a day. It's so dynamic, a short burst of sales can shoot a book toward the top. And that's what makes it fairly easy to create a bestseller on Amazon—or *rig* one, depending on your point of view.

True, Amazon is the world's biggest bookstore. But you'd need tons more sales to make the *New York Times* list, which is based on weekly sales from 4,000 bookstores and wholesalers serving another 60,000 retailers. With an Amazon Bestseller Campaign, however, you might simply line up 250 people to buy your book at 3 a.m. next Sunday, and you're No. 1. Sure, it's only for an hour, but you can put "bestselling author" on your resume for the rest of your life, right?

Well, let's get real. "Ranking high on Amazon certainly feels good, but it doesn't take many sales to achieve that," said Jacqueline Deval, publisher of Hearst Books and author of *Publicize Your Book.*

The problem is, Bestseller Campaigns are a seductive "quick fix" for authors who feel they don't have the time, energy or know-how for real grass-roots marketing. It's frustrating to pour your heart and soul into a book for months or years, and then have no one buy it. Amazon Bestseller Campaigns can sound like a good solution, simply because they promise instant success.

How Bestseller Campaigns work

The core of an Amazon Bestseller Campaign is an e-mail advertisement blasted to thousands of people. Some practitioners say it requires at least 300,000 messages to make any difference at all. People who get the e-mails are offered a one-time deal: a long list of "valuable free bonuses" like e-books, audio files of seminars, and other digital goodies, but only if they buy your book at Amazon on the day of your campaign.

The e-mail blasts are sent to registered subscribers of e-mail newsletters, so the messages aren't illegal spam. But just in case things don't go as well as planned, some consultants suggest you also pester your family, friends, and coworkers to buy your book on the special day to ensure it has enough sales to move up.

Plug Your Book! | 125

Books pushed with 'Bestseller' Campaigns

These books are touted as "Amazon Bestseller" success stories by the marketing consultants who helped launch the books. However, this look at their Amazon Sales Ranks reveals poor sales that became even weaker and more erratic over time. Peaks on the chart show periods of weak sales, valleys represent strong sales. **Conclusion: Sales can deteriorate badly for books marketed with special gimmicks.**

Success Bound: Breaking Free of Mediocrity by Gilbert (2001)

Best Rank: 20,973
Worst: 590,102
Average: 285,895

Nov 2004   Dec 2006

The Hidden Souls of Words by Garner (2004)

Best Rank: 40,493
Worst: 814,844
Average: 507,155

Jul 2005   Dec 2006

Mining Gold With an Offline Shovel by Christopher (2003)

Best Rank: 23,504
Worst: 662,305
Average: 324,897

Nov 2004   Dec 2006

Books plugged with online word of mouth

Word of mouth for these four books was established by the authors, using a Web site or blog. Notice the long-term trend is flat, indicating steady sales. **Conclusion: Books with Internet word of mouth can sell strongly year after year.**

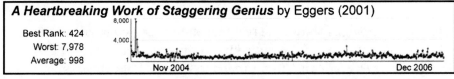

A Heartbreaking Work of Staggering Genius by Eggers (2001)

Best Rank: 424
Worst: 7,978
Average: 998

Nov 2004   Dec 2006

The Business of Writing for Children by Shepard (2000)

Best Rank: 1,027
Worst: 22,447
Average: 3,722

Nov 2004   Dec 2006

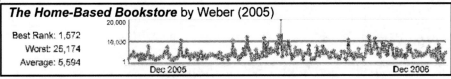

The Home-Based Bookstore by Weber (2005)

Best Rank: 1,572
Worst: 25,174
Average: 5,594

Dec 2005   Dec 2006

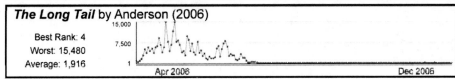

The Long Tail by Anderson (2006)

Best Rank: 4
Worst: 15,480
Average: 1,916

Apr 2006   Dec 2006

Charts provided by TitleZ.com, reprinted with permission. In some cases, charts don't extend all the way to back to the date of publication, when sales might have been strongest.

With some Bestseller Campaigns, buyers are offered many more freebies if they buy two, three, or even 20 copies of your book at the same time. The bonuses are advertised as being worth hundreds or even thousands of dollars.

... and this is success?

The marketing literature for Bestseller Campaigns gives plenty of references that seem to back up the promises. Dozens of earlier Bestseller Campaign books are listed as success stories. But a quick check of their actual sales on Amazon reveals that several of these books haven't been successful at all.

As shown in Figure 2.1, the sales charts for these books zigzag all over the place, a sure sign the book is going nowhere. Further, look at the sales ranks—they're a long, long way from No. 1. Obviously, these books are selling only a few copies a year on Amazon. If these are the success stories, the flameouts must be spectacular.

On the other hand, look at the three bottom sales charts in Figure 2.1, the ones for books promoted with Web sites and blogs. Their sales ranks are much stronger, and the trend lines are flat, meaning steady sales. These books probably sell more copies each day on Amazon than the "Bestsellers" rack up in a whole year.

Haywired Recommendations

What goes wrong with the Bestseller Campaign books? Some of them are probably wonderful books, but nobody's buying. Meanwhile, books with genuine word of mouth can have strong, steady sales for years.

A bit more digging into these Bestseller Campaigns shows the real reason they can collapse. When readers follow their own curiosity, they tend to buy lots of the same kinds of books. For example, the Amazon customer who buys *Andrew Jackson: His Life and Times* tends to buy the following books, in precisely this order:

> Team of Rivals: The Political Genius of Abraham Lincoln
>
> The Rise of American Democracy: Jefferson to Lincoln
>
> 1776
>
> His Excellency: George Washington
>
> The River of Doubt: Theodore Roosevelt's Darkest Journey

It's easy to see the connection, isn't it? These five titles are the Frequently Bought Together list, the guts of Amazon's recommendation engine. Customers who've bought only some of the books on the list soon receive recommendations for the rest in personalized e-mails or on the Web site. This results in tons of sales, and Amazon has it down to a science.

Bestseller Campaigns, however, throw a monkey wrench into this recommendation process. Instead of Amazon recommending similar books, it spits out unrelated books. For example, one Bestseller Campaign book, *Hidden Souls of Words*, is categorized Religion/Spirituality but its Frequently Bought Together list includes completely different kinds of books:

The Attractor Factor: 5 Easy Steps for Creating Wealth…

How to Be Wildly Wealthy FAST: A Step-by-Step Guide…

Turning Passions into Profits: Three Steps to Wealth and Power

The Biology of Belief: Unleashing the Power of Consciousness…

Life's Missing Instruction Manual: The Guidebook You Should…

What's the connection? There isn't any, except they're all Bestseller Campaign books. They were all pitched, high-pressure, perhaps to the same lists of people, no matter what their tastes in books. A few people bought, but some of them may have wanted the "valuable free bonuses," not the book.

And now we see the real problem: Amazon isn't recommending *Hidden Souls of Words* to anyone who actually might want to read it—people who like Religion/Spirituality books. This book's best chance at word of mouth is gone.

To be fair, a few of the Bestseller Campaign success stories really are bona-fide successes, including books by Gary Renard, Gary Rebstock, Dr. Bruce Lipton and Joe Vitale. Books by these authors sell year after year on Amazon, but is it because somebody ran an Amazon Bestseller Campaign? Or is it because these authors energetically promote their books year after year by blogging, writing articles, and giving interviews?

To be doubly fair, the consultants who advertise Amazon Bestseller Campaigns would surely tell you that a single technique doesn't support a book for long; steady sales depend on continuous promotion. Still, the question remains: Why do their clients actually fare so poorly?

Authors who ignite real word of mouth using techniques described in this book can draw a real audience who buys and recommends their book. But don't expect to hit the jackpot next month, if ever. Nothing in publishing is simple, easy and guaranteed.

Another problem with Bestseller Campaigns is the increasing unreliability of e-mail blasts. Despite laws against spam, junk e-mails are a growing problem. Increasingly, Internet Service Providers are deleting some e-mail blasts, even legitimate ones.

Is It Worth It?

It's pretty easy to do the math on Bestseller Campaigns. If you assume a cost of $2,700 and a profit on each book of $5, you'll need to sell 450 books to break even. (That's if you do the campaign yourself after taking the classes; if the consultant does it for you, it costs $15,000.)

The bigger question is, could your time and money be better spent sparking real word of mouth for your book?

If it's important to have a stellar Amazon Sales Rank for a day, you can do it much faster and cheaper by simply buying a few hundred copies of your book from Amazon yourself. Have a copy shipped to each member of your high-school class, your neighbors and in-laws, and every newspaper and magazine editor in your region. That would spark some *real* word of mouth for your book.

Beating people over the head isn't going to create demand for your book. Instead, create a way for readers to find you on their own. *That's* when you'll have an audience, and that's what this book is all about.

Ethics of Online Marketing

Perhaps nothing is more important to authors and publishers than their reputation. While it's perfectly fine to promote your work energetically, consider the way your promotion might appear to others. Sometimes there's a fine line between being aggressive and being overzealous.

In some cases, the boundaries are clear. For example, the CAN-SPAM Act outlawed unsolicited commercial e-mail, so it's inappropriate to market your book by sending e-mails to strangers. In other cases, you'll need to use your judgment. For example, one section of this book discusses how to persuade people to review your book on Amazon. But don't ask people who haven't read your book. And don't review your book yourself. Don't buy thousands of copies of your own book in a ploy to push it onto the bestseller list.

On the Internet, it's fairly easy to hide your identity, but often it comes back to haunt people who use it as a marketing technique.

Shill Reviews

For years it was rumored that several authors and publicists had posted flattering reviews of their own books on Amazon, anonymously. This dishonest tactic of writing shill reviews, sometimes called "astro-turfing," depends on contrived reviews to simulate a grassroots movement for a book on Amazon.

Then in 2004, a computer glitch revealed it was true—the real names of the authors were displayed, earning them a lifetime of embarrassment. One was John Rechy, author of the bestselling novel *City of Night*. The ironic thing was that Rechy was a successful writer whose honors included a PEN-USA West lifetime achievement award. He wasn't famous, but he didn't need shill book reviews either. But that computer glitch made him much better known, though probably not in the way he'd hoped.

One medical doctor who has a book for sale on Amazon has submitted hundreds of reviews of other books, which serve primarily to point attention to his own book. Apparently the doctor isn't concerned that his reputation as an author has been tarnished, as he's continued the activity.

In response to years of controversy about abuse of its review system, in 2006, Amazon began requiring that reviewers have an account with a registered credit card before reviews can be submitted. The safeguard prevents individuals from using multiple accounts to submit phony reviews. However, customers aren't required to purchase a copy of a book from Amazon before reviewing it.

Amazon recently began a program called "Amazon Verified Purchase," which means that the customer who wrote the review actually purchased the item at Amazon.com. This gives the review a bit more credibility and offers the consumer one more way to help gauge the quality and relevance of a product review. But if the review is not marked Amazon Verified Purchase, it doesn't mean that the reviewer has no experience with the product—just that he or she didn't buy it from Amazon.

When you write a new review on Amazon, you can mark your review as an Amazon Verified Purchase in the checkbox. If the checkbox doesn't appear, Amazon was unable to verify your purchase from them. If you wrote a review for a book you purchased at Amazon previously and would like to mark it as an Amazon Verified Purchase now, simply edit your existing review and the Amazon Verified Purchase checkbox should appear.

Spam

This book is intended to encourage authors to promote their book energetically and ethically. However, on the Internet, remember that tactics that may seem perfectly fine to you could offend someone else. For example, in 2005, an author sent a series of e-mails announcing his book to a list of addresses harvested from Amazon's Web site. Several recipients were angry enough to post critical reviews of the book and lambast the author for "spamming." The headline of the book's top "Most Helpful" review declares, "This author is a spammer." It's not something that will favorably impress potential readers.

Many book-marketing consultants advise authors to enter articles about themselves and their book in Wikipedia.org, the popular online encyclopedia. However, the site's guidelines clearly state that Wikipedia is not to be used for personal promotion or to popularize products or Web sites. Articles that are deemed self-promotional are deleted. Likewise, many books are promoted on Craigslist.com, an online classified service partially owned by eBay, in apparent violation of the site's terms of service.

Reputation is everything. A good marketer will plug his or her book relentlessly. But don't do something in the heat of the moment that could damage your credibility. The biggest asset authors and publishers have is their credibility with the public.

Consider the author we have already mentioned as being the first self-published author to hit 1 million eBook sales on Amazon, John Locke. His reputation as a best seller was tarnished when it came to light that he had used the services of GettingBookReviews.com, a now defunct service where authors paid to have people read and review their books. Although it happens all the time, as discussed in the earlier chapter "Getting Reviews," it is considered a breach of ethics for a reviewer to be paid for their opinion.

Todd Rutherford, the founder of GettingBookReviews.com, saw it differently. When he established his company, he felt he was meeting a real need for authors who struggled to have their fledgling books receive attention long enough to be reviewed. "I was creating reviews that pointed out the positive things, not the negative things," Rutherford said. "These were marketing reviews, not editorial reviews."

Rutherford saw them as blurbs, similar to the statements on the backs of books in the old days, when all books were physical objects and sold in stores. He claims he saw nothing unethical about hiring reviewers and encouraging them to deliver positive reviews.

Google, which had provided the advertising vehicle for Rutherford to attract reviewers, canceled his account when they recognized there might be an ethical problem—indeed, the U.S. Federal Trade Commission requires the publishers of online endorsements to disclose any such financial relationships, so that readers are alerted to the potential conflict of interest. Amazon cracked down on Rutherford, too, after the company received complaints that his reviews were the result of payments.

Whether the authors who signed up for Rutherford's service were aware of its pitfalls isn't clear. In any case, Rutherford was clearing $28,000 a month before his accounts at Amazon and Google were suspended.

Amazon's Official Kindle Direct Publishing Forum

As part of the Kindle Direct Publishing program, there is a helpful forum of writers helping writers. The Kindle Direct Publishing Forum home page states, "We have many accomplished authors and publishers who are very knowledgeable about all things "self-publishing with KDP" whose titles are currently selling in Amazon's Kindle Store. Ask for help from fellow authors or lend a hand to someone who is new to KDP."

Under the heading "Publisher Support," you may post questions about account and payment issues, and provide feedback to KDP. Under the heading "Ask the Community," you can ask questions of other, more experienced authors. Then there is a section called "Voice of the Author" which is a sort of general conversation forum for those in the KDP community. Here you can post threads about anything—from asking for manuscript help to venting about social issues. It's like a water cooler for writers who work at home. All Amazon asks is that you keep it clean.

https://kdp.amazon.com/community

Createspace Official Forum

While KDP is Amazon's self-publishing vehicle for authors selling eBooks, the company also has a unit that prints and sells paperback books called CreateSpace. As part of its service, Createspace maintains an online library of how-to articles, support forums, and other resources:

https://www.createspace.com

Click on "Free Publishing Resources," the blue tab at the top of the page, and have a look around. Of particular interest will be the helpful how-to's on how to correctly format your manuscript for whatever edition you are working with. You will also want to subscribe to their blog to be apprised of all the latest news in the world of publishing that you are becoming so intimately familiar with—or should be.

Your Action Plan

If you have read this book cover to cover, you're well equipped to handle your book's publicity on your own. But you may also be exhausted by the seemingly huge amount of work involved. That's why we've come up with this Action Plan for your book that you can use to structure your own efforts, make best use of your time, and guarantee that you touch the important bases and cross the easy proverbial T's.

Okay, so let's walk together through the publishing scenario. Whether your book is self-published or published by a traditional publisher, much of the post-publication publicity falls in your hands. And since everyone is different, these are just suggestions of the "how" and "when" to go about creating and increasing your book's publicity and online presence.

You may want to copy or tear out these pages and use them to cross off, like you might for a "To-Do" list. So here we go.

Snap a Photo of Your Book's Cover

A box of books arrives as your door. Rejoice! Your book-child is born. If you don't already have it, the first thing you want is a picture. You'll want a high- and low-resolution image of your book's front and back covers separately and together. And also a pdf of the cover. You will use these for many things over the next few months. File them in a folder called "Book Cover" or something like that.

Set Up Your Book's Facebook Page

Setting up a page for your book is probably the quickest and easiest way to get your book online in a public way. See Chapter 5 in this book for information on how to do this if you don't know already. Announce in your status update that that the book is available for sale and post a link to it on Amazon. Upload a jpeg of the front cover. Then upload a photo of the back cover. Then a photo of you. Create or find some art for your Cover page photo. It may take a day or two to get familiar with the differences between your personal page and your book's page with you as the administrator, but it's not that hard.

Fill In Your Amazon's Author Central Page

Here you'll be asked to do a few things, like post a short biography about yourself. We've described it in Chapter 1. It may take anywhere from a few hours to a few days to fill in the synopsis, summary, quotes and more, but it will be well worth it.

You can also use the "About the Author" page to tell an anecdote about your book and how you came to write it. If your book doesn't have an "inside flap," use that space for what you would have put on an inside flap if you had one. Usually, it's a short summary of the book.

The more you fill in here, the better. Review the last few pages of Chapter 1.

Create a Press Release

While we didn't specifically cover this in this book, a press release might be handy to have to forward to people when you're telling them about your book. It's another tool in your publicity shed.

You can research and read other press releases, but in general, it will provide the reader with the synopsis or summary of the book, without divulging the ending, a biography of the author (you can use the same copy you created for your Author Central Page), and maybe a preliminary review.

You probably have a lot of this information already. All you have to do is collect it and format it. This may take a few days to create.

Start Collecting Reviews

We've covered this in detail in this book. This is perhaps the most important tool for increasing your book publicity and creating sales for you book. The back and forth of this may take a few weeks to get going. When you send a book to someone, you might want to include your press release. Be sure to direct them to your Author Central Page at Amazon.com for more information on the book.

Create Some Marketing Buzz

Business cards, with the book's title and your contact information, are an easy way to market your book on a personal level. Picture yourself at a business function like a networking luncheon or at a party in your neighborhood or an event at your child's school. You're casually talking to the person next to you and you mention that you've just written a book. The next question is always, "What's the title of your book?" This person is genuinely interested but will, more often than not, forget the title ten minutes later. Hand them a business card. They are easy and inexpensive to produce and go right in the pocket or purse of the person you're talking to.

If you want to up the ante a little, have a post card made of your book. You can put the jpeg of your book's front cover on one side and post reviews on the other. But postcards are little billboards, not pocket reminders. When you hand them to people rather than mail them or stuff them into a bag, people won't know what to do with them.

If you make a postcard and put a review on it, be sure to ask permission of the reviewer before you print and hand out these cards. When quotes are used for promotional purposes, you need permission. If your book is relevant to them, charity groups may be happy to include your postcard in their "goody" bags at events. But you'll need to seek permission first, and many charge a small fee for inclusion.

Both business cards and postcards can be printed on demand and within a day, once you know what you want on them.

Start Blogging

If you don't already have a blog, now is the time to decide whether you want one and whether it should be a part of your website. We talk about blogs in this book, so re-read that chapter. A blog is a very important tool for connecting with readers, creating content for social media, and putting you on the road to become an expert spokesperson about your topic and book.

You might also consider writing an article about your book and offering it to a website that attracts people who might be interested in your book's subject. Most of these sites don't pay for articles but the exposure can be great.

From your decision to start a blog to getting your blog up and running can take anywhere from a day to eternity. So get going on both the content and the technology.

Build Your Web Presence

While you may see ads for "build your website in 30 minutes," or something like that, websites take a little more time and need to be thought out a little. Plus, there can be a learning curve. This isn't to say that they can't be done in a few days. All we're saying is that you might want to get your Facebook page up first, and then your blog before you move to the website. You may also want to hire someone to help you with the site.

Get Social

From your blog, website, press release, and reviews, you should now have some content to post on your social media sites. Whether you chose Facebook, Pinterest or Twitter, these posts works best when you post short and important tips, quotes or sentences from your book. Go back and review what works and doesn't. But do make a 30-day or 90-day plan for promoting your book on Facebook and attach it to a calendar so you are prompted every few days to do something.

Listen Up

Once you get your online presence set up, concentrate on your audio and video presence. Schedule some interviews, edit some podcasts, post some clips. Again, your objective now is to create content around your book with you as the author, authority and expert.

Advance Your Tools

Go back to your Amazon Author Central page and work on Shelfari, List Mania, See Inside, Buy X Get Y, LibraryThing, GoodReads, and more. There's a lot in this book that you can drill down to. Now is the time.

Refresh Yourself!

Just when you think you're done, go back and refresh everything. Book sales compound month after month and while it's true that most of your publicity will happen around your book's release date and within the few months after, a book can peak years later. So refresh, refresh, refresh. Write a new article or blog, or find some way to make you and your book relevant to today's news. And post, post, post.

INDEX

CPSIA information can be obtained at www.ICGtesting.com
Printed in the USA
BVOW03s0152260515

401615BV00007B/113/P

9 781936 560158